Endowment Management for Higher Education

Second Edition

By Nicole Wellmann Kraus

With Valentina Glaviano and Jay A. Yoder

1133 20th Street NW, Suite 300, Washington, DC 20036

About AGB

The Association of Governing Boards of Universities and Colleges (AGB) is the premier membership organization that strengthens higher education governing boards and the strategic roles they serve within their organizations. Through our vast library of resources, educational events, and consulting services, and with nearly 100 years of experience, we empower 40,000 AGB members from more than 2,000 institutions and foundations to navigate complex issues, implement leading practices, streamline operations, and govern with confidence. AGB is the trusted resource for board members, chief executives, and key administrators on higher education governance and leadership. For more information, visit www.AGB.org.

1001 19th Street North, 17th Floor, Arlington, VA 22209

About Strategic

Strategic Investment Group (Strategic) was founded in 1987 by the senior members of the investment office managing the World Bank's multibillion-dollar portfolio. They understood the complex and difficult role of a fiduciary and as a result, founded a firm intended to be a fiduciary partner, or investment office for hire, for a select number of clients. The organization was built with the vision to provide sophisticated, customized investment solutions for clients, which were traditionally only available to multibillion-dollar investors, allowing all clients to gain the benefits of our best ideas. A pioneer of the dedicated Outsourced Chief Investment Officer (OCIO) model, Strategic's mission is to provide the same type of comprehensive customized fiduciary investment solutions to organizations that do not choose to, or do not have the ability to, build this capability internally. This frees clients from the day-to-day business of managing investment portfolios so that they can focus on their core mission. We become our client's investment office and function seamlessly as an extension of their staff. For more information, visit www.strategicgroup.com.

Printed in the United States of America.
ISBN 978-1-951635-21-3
ISBN 978-1-951635-22-0 (ePub)
ISBN 978-1-951635-23-7 (Kindle)

Contents

Acknowledgments

We greatly appreciate our colleagues at AGB, who provided the opportunity to work on this project with them, and to do it again in this revised, second edition.

Our understandings of endowment management have evolved by working with excellent committees over the years. A special thank-you to all the clients we have had the pleasure of serving and working alongside to fulfill their investment goals. We would like to thank our colleagues and former colleagues at Strategic Investment Group, where there are many great opportunities to hone our craft. Hilda Brillembourg-Ochoa, Michael Bishop, David Ordoobadi, Tim O'Hara, and Ken Grossfield—valued colleagues and gifted writers—were invaluable resources, and we offer a special thank you to Brian Murdock for his support.

We offer a heartfelt thank-you to Charley Ellis, the former chair of the Yale Investment Committee and author of the Afterword in the first edition, whose generosity, encouragement, guidance, and willingness to read many versions of the first edition over a number of months made it much more valuable. The feedback from Clint Stevenson and Cathleen Rittereiser was profoundly helpful. David Bass provided helpful feedback on this new edition, and graciously agreed to pen the Foreword.

Our families are the ultimate gifts to us, and we would like to thank our supportive families and friends, who provided inspiration as well as inestimable help with the extra hours required to complete this labor of love.

Foreword

Endowments are a long-established philanthropic model, providing educational institutions with dedicated pools of assets that serve as perpetual funding for programs, faculty positions, scholarships, and other purposes, while also affording donors a means of segregating gifted assets from other institutional funds to ensure that their philanthropic purposes are fulfilled in perpetuity. Modern endowments are also powerful financial tools, leveraging immensely complex investment strategies to maintain and grow philanthropic resources even as other institutional revenue sources decline. Effective endowment management similarly starts with fundamental principles of trusteeship (integrity, independence of thought and collective decision-making, a focus on long-term strategy and sustainability) but requires sophisticated policies and practices informed by the expertise and wisdom of board members, staff, and investment service providers.

Since this book was last revised in 2017, the COVID-19 pandemic underscored both the critical role endowments play in institutional finances, and the importance of setting and adhering to prudent endowment management policies. During the first year of the pandemic, many institutions experienced steep drops in tuition and other operating revenue and incurred unplanned expenses. While endowment funds cannot close such budget gaps, they can buffer the impact of financial crises, enabling institutions to maintain funding for student financial aid and other critical purposes. The year delivered a reminder that endowment management requires a steady hand and solid policy. After precipitous declines in the first quarter of 2020, investment markets quickly rebounded, growing to record highs by the end of the calendar year. Investment committees that adhered to prudent polices could celebrate a record year. Boards that abandoned policy or tried to time the market likely eroded the value of the portfolios under their management for years to come.

The year 2020 also highlighted growing disparities in institutions' wealth, financial sustainability, and ability to provide equitable opportunities and outcomes for students, raising questions about the ways higher education both perpetuates and mitigates these long-standing disparities. The Black Lives Matter movement galvanized interest in how philanthropy and investment practices align with institutional commitments to racial equity and social justice. Boards are, and will continue to be, challenged to make endowment management more diverse and inclusive, and ensure that investments align with institutional missions and values.

The second edition of *Endowment Management for Higher Education* provides a comprehensive overview of endowment management for governing boards of colleges, universities, and institutionally related foundations, outlining fundamental fiduciary responsibilities as they relate to endowment management, current best practices in investment and spending policy, portfolio construction, and guidance on management models and staffing. Among numerous other updates, this edition includes a new chapter on aligning the endowment portfolio with institutional mission and the incorporation of environmental, social, and governance (ESG) values into endowment management.

AGB owes a debt of gratitude to Nicole Wellmann Kraus and Valentina Glaviano for their work on this new edition of the book and to Strategic Investment Group, whose commitment and support made it possible. Having worked closely with dozens of investment committees over more than two decades, their guidance is informed by both technical expertise and a profound understanding of the ways board policy, culture, and dynamics contribute to effective endowment stewardship. In a period in which colleges and universities are facing enormous challenges and undergoing significant changes, we are delighted to provide boards with this valuable guide to prudent investment management and a reminder of the very long-term impact their work will have on the students, institutions, and communities they serve.

David Bass
Executive Director, Philanthropic Governance
Association of Governing Boards of Universities and Colleges
January 2022

Introduction

The volunteers who serve on the investment committees of boards of higher education institutions, institutionally related foundations and certain institution investment corporations assume important fiduciary responsibilities. Their challenge is to help secure the future of their colleges and universities by managing their endowments wisely. They also undertake the important social role of preserving intergenerational equity, ensuring that today's students and future students benefit equally from the endowments. This book is dedicated to these volunteers' service. It has been written in the hope of providing guidance to facilitate their effective stewardship of the endowments underpinning our colleges and universities.

Society attaches ever-increasing value to educational attainment. At the same time, rising costs in higher education amplify the pressure on the investment committees of public and independent colleges to boost their investment returns. Endowments are an increasingly precious resource to cover rising costs, strengthen financial resilience, support important initiatives, and provide financial aid to students and budgetary support to help keep higher education affordable. The work of a college or university investment committee member has never been more important. The future of access to and excellence in higher education is at stake.

Market returns since the Great Financial Crisis have been higher than average. These unusually high returns were accompanied by a greater ability of some students to pay for tuition, increased capacity of donors to contribute to endowments, and the stronger overall financial health of higher education institutions. These favorable developments came to an abrupt end with the emergence of the COVID-19 pandemic. The severe disruption and uncertainty unleashed by the pandemic have caused major setbacks for many institutions. While the economic and market impact of the pandemic was relatively short-lived, there will be lingering scars from the pandemic's dramatic impact on economic activity and human behavior. Many institutions will also likely bear scars that will take time to heal. The pandemic should serve as a wake-up call to all about the precarious footing on which many institutions operate. The darkest periods of the pandemic revealed the vulnerability of both our endowments and our operations, and underscored the need to redouble our efforts to increase the resilience of the institutions we serve.

Husbanding endowment resources through complicated and unforgiving times in financial markets presents a whole set of additional challenges. For years, an 8 or 9 percent return on endowments has been commonly used in long-term budget plans. However, many members of investment committees believe that it will be more difficult going forward to generate the level of investment returns required to preserve intergenerational equity. This undertaking was best defined by economist and Nobel laureate James Tobin, who aptly noted: "The trustees of an endowed institution are the guardians of the future against the claims of the present. Their task is to preserve equity among generations." Markets are becoming increasingly complex, and in slower-growth markets, more modest investment returns will be generated. Opportunities to beat the market are growing scarcer while the opportunities for costly missteps mount. Access to compelling managers continues to prove important to generate the returns needed, and the smallest institutions have an additional challenge that their portfolios are often not large enough to get the attention of the managers who could generate distinguished returns.

Yet growing endowments are indispensable to maintaining higher education as we know it. Current budgetary outlays rely on regular transfers from the endowment, and an increasing number of students rely on endowed scholarships, while the long-term financial viability of universities and colleges depends on preserving and increasing endowment resources. Without endowments to help defray ever-rising costs, higher education would be an unattainable dream for many talented young people. Endowments need the benefit of the board's guidance to meet the current demands placed on them and their long-term goal of providing a growing resource of support to the institution into the future.

The challenges of investing are both technical and human. To excel, endowment stewards must be as attentive to landmines in governance as they are to those in global markets. Stories abound of institutions with brilliant technical investment processes but poor governance practices that undermined the work of their investment teams.

Given all these challenges, those agreeing to serve on investment committees shoulder important responsibilities. Yet the emotional rewards are also great. Helping to expand the endowment of an alma mater or another beloved institution, and thus helping to secure its future, can be a source of great pride.

This book is a new edition of *Endowment Management for Higher Education*, published in 2017. This new edition includes additional observations gleaned from the authors' combined nine decades of working with investment committees. In particular, we have included an entirely new chapter on environmental, social, and governance (ESG) investing given the emphasis that many are placing on mission- and values-oriented investments.

Unfortunately, markets continue to teach painful lessons for all types of investors, including those charged with protecting and increasing institutional endowments. Drawing on our experience as well as insights shaped by this tumultuous era, the authors hope that this book will be useful for any member of an investment committee.

Before delving into the intricacies of endowment management, the following list reviews some of the important lessons of recent years, including those born of the COVID-19 crisis:

- *Many investment committees do not accurately assess their tolerance for risk.* Some committees may take too much risk (only to subsequently be forced to unwind it at an inopportune time), while others may take too little risk, creating significant opportunity costs. Additionally, after periods of sustained market highs, humans often overestimate their tolerance for risk or return volatility. Often, a lack of communication and coordination between a board's finance and investment committees prevents the development of an integrated "enterprise risk management" approach that considers the overall operating, financial, and investment risks of the institution rather than the suboptimal approach of assessing each in isolation. COVID-19 exposed these weaknesses in many organizations.
- *Maintaining appropriate liquidity is critical.* There is a risk that institutions undervalue liquidity and find themselves unable to meet liquidity requirements for their institutions. As John Maynard Keynes so famously observed, "The market can stay irrational longer than you can stay solvent."
- *Creating asset tranches based on the anticipated use and the time horizon of funds can be valuable from a behavioral standpoint in creating discipline for boards.* These arrangements ensure that adequate liquidity has been set aside to meet anticipated budgetary needs for a few years. Those institutions that had set aside assets earmarked for near-term use in this way gave comfort that budgetary needs would be met despite the steep declines in asset values experienced during the COVID-19 crisis.
- *Many institutions seek to emulate others and focus too much on the investment strategies followed by a few large universities.* This focus misses the essential point that the strategies pursued by each investment committee must be tailored to its particular institution's circumstances, capabilities, and long-run strategic goals. The additional flexibility and organizational strength that the largest, wealthiest institutions have due to their balance sheets and competitive positioning should not be underestimated. Only institutions with access to top-tier investment talent—internally or through an outside advisor—should even consider this model; other institutional leaders must be more aware of their budgetary needs and level of dependence on the endowment.
- *Operational due diligence is critical.* While it is vital to understand each portfolio manager's investment process and performance, cases of fraud and other scandals involving "investment" firms have made an entirely new level of due diligence—known as operational due diligence—a best practice for all investment programs.
- *Leadership is critical.* The leaders of investment committees must understand that their institutions' futures may depend on the success of this committee. The best investment committee chairs act as servant leaders who ensure each member of their committee participates appropriately. Each member of the investment committee must be up to the task. This goes to the heart of the mission of the Association of Governing Boards of Universities and Colleges

(AGB). Each member must have the requisite skills and judgment and dedicate the necessary time to fulfill his or her obligations. This makes recruitment and vetting of prospective committee members a high priority. If warranted, failure to perform may lead to the removal of a committee member. It is far better to avoid this circumstance by fully informing potential candidates of the duties of committee members and the time and energy commitment before they accept.

- *Communication about the investment program among senior officials—including the chair of the board, the chair of the investment committee, the head of institutional development, the president and the chief financial officer—must be frequent and clear.* This is equally true for independent institutions and for public institutions that may have separate foundation boards. The early involvement of all key leaders in certain strategic decisions regarding asset allocation, spending policy, and risk tolerance can be crucial. If any of these officials lose faith in the investment program at the wrong time, they may instigate changes that can wreak havoc on investment returns.

- *Institutional memory should be valued and preserved.* The stability of the investment committee's membership is important. Meeting minutes are also critically important to preserving institutional memory—key decisions, and the reasons for them, should be documented and referenced when issues resurface.

- *There is tremendous momentum to promote diversity, equity, and inclusion (DEI) in manager selection. There are also increasing initiatives to improve DEI within the investment management industry, and to implement investment practices that focus on ESG.* The emphasis we place on DEI and ESG on our campuses has become an increased focus for our portfolios. This process also needs great stewardship and guidance by the board, which is why we have added a new chapter (4) dedicated to the ideal steps to take to make sure you arrive at the right place for your institution.

We are honored to partner with the AGB to bring you this new edition of the book. We encourage all board and committee members to avail themselves of AGB's excellent publications and conferences, information about which can be found at AGB.org. Each member of an institution's board has important obligations in carrying out the work of the full board and its committees. While this book focuses on the work of the investment committee, no single work can encompass every aspect of endowment management. There have been many excellent books published on the subject; in an appendix, we have provided a list of works that we consider essential reading for every member of an investment committee. Serving on an investment committee should be undertaken with as much information and preparation as possible. We trust this book will provide useful guidance to both new and experienced investment committee members.

Chapter 1

The Institutional Endowment

Understanding how the endowment fits into the mix of the costs, revenues, assets, and liabilities of the college, university, and foundation is a key first step in designing the central decision-making guide for investment committees: the investment policy. The targeted investment return and risk the institution accepts must be guided by the evolving role of the endowment in supporting the mission and finances of the institution. The investment and spending policies of the endowment must balance current and long-term budgetary needs, support the strategic direction of the institution, and comply with both regulatory requirements and best practices. We begin by defining the term "endowment," then discuss the duties and responsibilities of a fiduciary before turning to the historical context in which endowments evolved. Subsequently, this chapter discusses operating budgets, spending policy, and the pivotal role of gifts and donations in growing endowments over time.

Definition

Endowments are pools of institutional funds accumulated from donations, operating surpluses, and other revenue sources. Most donations to endowments are intended to support educational purposes such as scholarships, faculty support, and capital expenses, and are legally restricted as to their use. Funds such as operating surpluses may be added to the endowment by the board of trustees and are usually unrestricted. Taken together, endowment funds are governed by the board and are managed with a long-term horizon.

Fiduciary Responsibilities

A fiduciary generally is defined as someone acting in a position of trust on behalf of, or for the benefit of, a third party. Boards of trustees, investment committees, and professional investment staff of colleges and universities are all fiduciaries. The duties of these actors have evolved over the years with the adoption of several acts and regulations applicable to specific types of fiduciaries.

The chief responsibilities of a fiduciary are care, loyalty, and obedience.

Care. Standards of reasonable care have evolved over time. The well-known "prudent man" rule was first pronounced by Samuel Putnam, justice of the Massachusetts Supreme Judicial Court, in *Harvard College v. Amory* (1830): "All that can be required of a trustee to invest is, that he shall conduct himself faithfully and exercise a sound discretion. He is to observe how men of prudence, discretion, and intelligence manage their own affairs, not in regard to speculation, but in regard to the permanent disposition of their funds, considering the probable income, as well as the probable safety of the capital to be invested." The evolution of this standard as it relates to endowment fiduciaries is discussed below.

An excellent document on fiduciary responsibility, the *AGB Board of Directors' Statement on the Fiduciary Duties of Governing Board Members* (2015) should be read by every board member. It notes that "Fiduciary principles and duties are at the heart of effective governance and AGB's work with its members. . . . What could be more essential for a board member than to act with good faith and care, with loyalty to the institution, and in compliance with its mission and the law? And yet, behind nearly every failure of governance and leadership at higher education institutions is a breach of the principles of fiduciary duty."

Loyalty. Undivided loyalty requires that a fiduciary discharge his or her duties solely and exclusively in the interests of the beneficiary. Any action designed to advantage the fiduciary or anyone else—rather than the beneficiary—violates the duty of loyalty. Therefore, managing conflicts of interest is essential to meeting the loyalty standard. The duty of loyalty is an absolute standard.

Obedience. Endowment fiduciaries have a duty to remain faithful to the goals of the college or university (as set forth in its governing documents), foundation goals of a college or university and the mission of the foundation if applicable, and to ensure that the endowment is operating in compliance with applicable laws and regulations. When dealing with gifts, the Uniform Prudent Management of Institutional Funds Act (UPMIFA) outlines the duty of obedience and also dictates compliance with donor intent regarding the use of funds as well as spending and preservation of the fund. We would suggest that it is best practice for your board to receive an annual review of these relevant laws and regulations in order to best discharge these important duties.

Managing Conflicts of Interest

The fiduciary duty of loyalty dictates that board members act in the best interest of the institution and those decisions are made without personal economic conflict. While boards much be attentive to and appropriately manage potential conflicts of interest for all members, investment committees should be particularly diligent. The *AGB Board of Directors' Statement on Conflict of Interest with Guidance on Compelling Benefit* (2013) suggests that "boards should consider whether to adopt conflict of interest policies that specifically address board members' parallel or 'side-by-side' investments in which the institution has a financial interest" and also "whether to adopt especially rigorous conflict of interest provisions applicable to members of the board investment committee." AGB's Statement outlines 12 principles to manage potential conflicts of interest including those which might seem justified by some "compelling benefit" that accrues to the institution as a result of the potentially conflicted relationship:

1. Each board must bear ultimate responsibility for the terms and administration of its conflict-of-interest policy. Although institutional officers, staff, and legal counsel can assist in administration of the policy, boards should be sensitive to the risk that the judgment of such persons may be impaired by their roles relative to the board's.

2. We believe that the following standard properly gauges whether a board member's actual or apparent conflict of interest should be permissible, with or without (as the situation warrants) institutional management of the conflict:

   (a) If reasonable observers, having knowledge of all the relevant circumstances, would conclude that the board member has an actual or apparent conflict of interest in a matter related to the institution, the board member should have no role for the institution in the matter.

   (b) If, however, involvement by the board member would bring such compelling benefit to the institution that the board should consider whether to approve involvement, any decision to approve involvement should be subject to carefully defined conditions that assure both propriety and the appearance of propriety.

3. (a) When a board member is barred by actual or apparent conflict of interest from voting on a matter, ordinarily the board member should not participate in or attend board discussion of the matter, even if to do so would be legally permissible. (b) If, however, the board determines that it would significantly serve the interests of the board to have the conflicted board member explain the issue or answer questions, the board, if legally free to do so, may consider whether to invite the board member for that limited purpose. Any resulting invitation should be recorded in the minutes of the meeting.

4. A board should not confine its conflict-of-interest policy to financial conflicts, but should instead extend that policy to all kinds of interests that may (a) lead a board member to advance an initiative that is incompatible with the board member's fiduciary duty to the institution, or (b) entail steps by the board member to achieve personal gain, or gain to family, friends or associates, by apparent use of the board member's role at the institution.

5. Board members should be required to disclose promptly all situations that involve actual or apparent conflicts of interest related to the institution as the situations become known to them. To facilitate board members' identification of such conflicts, institutions should take affirmative steps at least annually to inform their board members of major institutional relationships and transactions, so as to maximize awareness of possible conflicts.

6. Board members should be required to disclose not less often than annually interests known by them to entail potential conflict of interest.

7. At institutions that receive substantial federal research funding, financial thresholds for mandatory disclosure of board members' conflicts of interest should not be higher than the thresholds then in effect that regulate conflicts of interest by faculty engaged in federally sponsored research. Boards of institutions that do not receive substantial federal research funding should take into account the federal sponsorship-related thresholds in determining thresholds for mandatory disclosure of board member conflicts of interest.

8. Interests of a board member's dependent children, and of members of a board member's immediate household, should be disclosed and regulated by the conflict-of-interest policy applicable to board members in the same manner as are conflicts of the board member.

9. Institutional policy on board member conflicts of interest should extend to the activities of board committees and should apply to all committee members, including those who are not board members.

10. Boards should consider whether to adopt conflict of interest policies that specifically address board members' parallel or "side-by-side" investments in which the institution has a financial interest.

11. Boards should also consider whether to adopt especially rigorous conflict of interest provisions applicable to members of the board investment committee.

12. To the extent that the foregoing recommendations exceed but are not inconsistent with state law requirements applicable to members of public college and public university boards, such boards should voluntarily adopt the recommendations.

Historical Framework

At one time, the term "endowment" was associated only with America's wealthiest and most prestigious institutions. Today, most of the nation's public and independent colleges and universities depend, to varying degrees, on their endowments and the spending policies that govern annual distributions.

The modern concept of "endowment" originated hundreds of years ago, most notably in England during the Middle Ages, when wealthy landowners donated land to religious groups, which in turn used the rental income for charitable purposes. Traditionally managed under the dictates of English trust law, it wasn't until the latter half of the 20th century that endowments began to be governed by a new set of legal principles and practices. These new standards were defined in a 1969 report to the Ford Foundation, *Managing Educational Endowments*, authored by the Advisory Committee on Endowment Management chaired by Robert Barker, a prominent trustee and investment manager. At that time, the Ford Foundation was a significant contributor to educational endowments and had found that they were poorly managed, generating returns well below equity market indices. Added to other studies and reports issued at the time, the "Barker Report," as it became known, transformed the modern practice of endowment management. As the report states:

> The ultimate responsibility for managing college and university endowments belongs, of course, to their trustees. Thus, it is not surprising that during the last few decades, endowment management has been dominated by some powerful traditional attitudes on the part of trustees. These attitudes have been the almost inevitable product of earlier experience. They have centered on safety and income rather than on seeking maximum total return. The result has been a series of largely unrecognized constraints on endowment management that have been costly as a result of changing social and economic conditions.

Historically, fiduciaries for nonprofit organizations, including endowments, generally looked to the common law of trusts to guide their investment and spending decisions. However, these laws, which generally allowed spending only from the "income" generated by the organizations' investments, often resulted in portfolios that focused on yield rather than on total return. These laws also forced fiduciaries to analyze risk on an investment-by-investment basis, rather than at the total portfolio level, and they did not permit the delegation of investment authority.

In 1972, the National Conference of Commissioners on Uniform State Laws enacted the Uniform Management of Institutional Funds Act (UMIFA), which replaced some of the specific restrictions imposed by common law with a more general prudence standard. UMIFA's enactment released colleges and universities from the constraining division of income and capital gains and allowed them to benefit from total-return investing. It also allowed for delegation of investment authority both to committees of a governing board and to independent investment advisors.

Underwater endowment funds

Many institutions have not had to worry about an underwater endowment fund for some time, yet CASE collaborated with AGB and Strategic Investment Group to produce the report *Fundraising and Endowment Resilience: Lessons for Leadership* (CASE, 2021) and in it, noted that:

> As with a general endowment spending policy, a board policy addressing spending from underwater endowment funds can help ensure that spending decisions are not unduly influenced by short-term pressures to distribute funds that may have long-term consequences for fund values. Policy approaches may include the following provisions for spending from underwater funds:
>
> - Discontinuation of all distributions,
> - Distribution of only interest and dividends,
> - Continuation of normal distributions until funds fall to some threshold below HDV (e.g., 90 percent below the value at which the fund was created),
> - A calibrated approach in which distributions are reduced by incremental amounts at various thresholds below HDV.
>
> Policies may also allow for different spending practices based on account purposes (e.g., continuing distributions supporting currently enrolled students but discontinuing endowed scholarships for an upcoming year that have yet to be awarded) or determining spending practices on a case-by-case basis in light of the seven factors outlined above.
>
> Respondents to the June 2020 survey of chief advancement officers found a wide spectrum of approaches. Worryingly, 17 percent of CAOs did not know about board policies for spending from underwater funds. Also of concern is the proportion of institutions (22 percent) making decisions on a case-by-case basis. One of the benefits of a prescriptive policy is that if it helps boards stay the course in challenging times. While some extraordinary funds may require individual board attention, few boards have the time to make case-by-case spending decisions for hundreds or thousands of individual endowment accounts.

In 2006, UMIFA was replaced with the Uniform Prudent Management of Institutional Funds Act (UPMIFA). Among other changes, UPMIFA refined and strengthened the standard of care applicable to fiduciaries, requiring them to act "with the care an ordinarily prudent person in a like position would exercise under similar circumstances," and to consider specific factors—such as general economic conditions, expected tax consequences of an investment, the role that each investment plays within the overall investment portfolio, the other resources of the institution, and the needs of the institution—in order to make distributions and to preserve capital. In addition, whereas under UMIFA, an "underwater endowment fund" (i.e., an endowment whose market value is less than its historic dollar value) could distribute only current income (e.g., dividends and interest), UPMIFA permits an endowment to distribute the amount that its fiduciaries deem prudent after considering donor intent, the purposes of the endowment, and other enumerated factors. UPMIFA has been adopted by 49 states and the District of Columbia. The requirements of a given state's UPMIFA statute should be understood by the governing board and investment committee members as they make important investment and spending decisions. For a summary and overview of UPMIFA, see David Bass, *Spending and Management of Endowments under UPMIFA* (AGB, 2010).

UPMIFA—as well as the Uniform Prudent Investor Act (UPIA), which is applicable to trust fiduciaries and overlaps considerably with UPMIFA—reflects the significant changes that have occurred in the investment practices of fiduciaries during the more than 30 years that followed the initial adoption of UMIFA. There are three notable developments codified by UPMIFA:

- Fiduciaries are required to diversify the investment portfolio. UPMIFA states that "an institution shall diversify the investments of an institutional fund unless the institution reasonably determines that, because of special circumstances, the purposes of the fund are better served without diversification." Diversification is not merely a good idea, but it is required by law in most cases.
- Fiduciaries are required to focus on the risk/reward characteristics of the total portfolio. UPMIFA provides that "[m]anagement and investment decisions about an individual asset must be made not in isolation but rather in the context of the institutional fund's portfolio of investments as a whole and as a part of an overall investment strategy having risk and return objectives reasonably suited to the fund and to the institution." The act further states that an institution "may invest in any kind of property or type of investment" to the extent consistent with these principles.
- Fiduciaries are permitted—even encouraged—to delegate investment and management functions. This point is often widely misunderstood, but in fact, UPMIFA empowers fiduciaries to ". . . delegate to an external agent the management and investment of an institutional fund to the extent that an institution could prudently delegate under the circumstances." UPMIFA describes the standards applicable to the appointment and monitoring of any delegatee, and notes that an institution that follows those standards ". . . is not liable for the decisions or actions of an agent to which the function was delegated." Because investing an endowment or any large pool of money is a complex and specialized task requiring full-time professional attention, we would argue that fiduciaries may even be required to delegate responsibilities, whether to an internal investment office, a consultant, or an outsourced chief investment officer (OCIO).

Although the Employee Retirement Income Security Act of 1974 (ERISA) applies only to pension plans, it provides additional context for what is expected of fiduciaries. As the U.S. Supreme Court noted in 2015 in *Tibble v. Edison*, the duties of an ERISA fiduciary (not to mention the fiduciary duties under UPIA, and, by extension, UPMIFA), are derived from the same source—the common law of trusts. In addition, some endowment fiduciaries may also serve as fiduciaries to pension plans maintained by the sponsoring institution, in which case the ERISA standards would be directly applicable.

Often, when discussing the fiduciary duties owed to an endowment, the focus is on investment decisions made (i.e., buys and sells). However, it is important to remember that holding an investment is itself an investment decision and, consequently, the monitoring of that investment is also an integral part of one's fiduciary duty. The Supreme Court in *Tibble* made this clear in a brief survey of trust law on this subject. The court noted that a fiduciary has a continuing duty to monitor investments, which exists "separate and apart from the trustee's duty to exercise prudence in selecting investments at the outset." This point is revisited in the discussion of the key duties of the investment committee in chapter 2.

While a sound decision-making process is fundamental to the fulfillment of a board's or committee's fiduciary duty, it is also crucial that this process be well-documented. Not only will records of deliberations and investment decisions, including the increasingly common decisions around aligning portfolio with mission and values, provide valuable context and institutional history to newly appointed members of these bodies, but they could also prove to be valuable insurance against claims of imprudence in the event that an investment decision performs poorly. In fact, documenting a proper process is almost as important as the decision itself.[1] Given the importance of this obligation, we will devote further attention to it in chapter 2.

UPMIFA: Questions Boards Should Be Asking

- Are we familiar with our state's UPMIFA statue?
- Can we confidently affirm that endowed funds are only expended in ways that fully comply with donor intent and that expendable funds are not allowed to accumulate unspent?
- Do we honor the specific terms of gift instruments in regard to spending or accumulation of individual endowment funds?
- Do we have confidence in our projections regarding the long-term purchasing power of endowment funds?
- Do we have a formal policy addressing spending from underwater endowments that is compliant with UPMIFA?
- Do we have a process in place to identify individual endowment funds in danger of falling below their original value (historic dollar value) and monitor underwater funds?
- Does the institution work with donors to determine alternate uses for funds that may have become impossible, imprudent, or illegal to fulfill or, absent living donors, identify alternate uses for such funds? (Some state UPMIFA statutes allow institutions to repurpose older and smaller funds when it is no longer practicable or possible to fulfill them. In other cases, foundations may have to petition the state attorney general to repurpose funds.)

Operating-Budget Mix

Historically, most public colleges and universities have had an operating budget supported by three primary sources of funding: tuition and student fees, gifts, and state support. Yes, they have investment income, but it traditionally does not contribute a great deal as a percentage of the operating budget. Independent institutions rely on tuition, gifts, and investment income as the primary sources of their revenue. Some publics and independents also receive sizable research grants. For public institutions that receive state appropriations, that support has declined markedly, leading in some cases, to sharp tuition increases. Consider the case of one midwestern college with which the authors are familiar. Its state support has declined from more than 60 percent of the operating budget to a little over 30 percent in fewer than 15 years. Many other public institutions, which educate the vast majority of postsecondary students in this country, face similar challenges. Given this environment, many institutions have dedicated more of their boards' time to strategizing about ways to diversify this revenue mix through adding or expanding such resources as intellectual-property royalties and rental income. Finally, growing the endowment is essential for many institutions' survival, and contributions from endowments could make up a larger portion of the operating budget of such institutions in the coming decades.

More money, if allocated and employed wisely, can enhance educational excellence and provide a competitive advantage over an institution's peers, not to mention providing scholarship support to students who otherwise could not afford to attend. Even a cursory look at the *U.S. News & World Report* rankings of colleges and universities makes clear the correlation between rankings and endowment size. Financial resources per student have been assigned around a 10 percent weighting in calculating the rankings—far less than the roughly 20 percent assigned to academic reputation and 20 percent to faculty resources—but the latter two measures are heavily dependent on the first.

An endowment affords donors an opportunity to make substantial gifts that will benefit an institution and its students in perpetuity. This characteristically—almost uniquely—American charitable impulse is a driving force in the creation and growth of endowments that will benefit generations to come.

In short, a large and growing endowment contributes to financial resilience, provides opportunities for renewing and expanding facilities and programs, and most importantly for many colleges, educating all students—regardless of their ability to pay. Many institutions feel that ensuring equal access and opportunities for success for students regardless of their financial means is an important element of their mission. Assuming that money is allocated and spent wisely, numerous competitive advantages will accrue to the institution's benefit and—more importantly—to the benefit of its current and future students and faculty, whose satisfaction adds to the quality of the educational experience.

Spending Policy

Spending policy governs the appropriate level of resources that may be distributed from an endowment and how those resources will be utilized within an institution's operating budget. One of the institutional governing board's most important responsibilities, chiefly decided by the finance committee with consultation with the investment committee, is deciding how much to spend from the endowment. Real growth of the endowment requires that the assets outperform inflation and spending. In addition, the spending policy must strive to achieve intergenerational equity, so that tomorrow's students benefit as much as today's. There is often a natural tension between decisions to maximize the experience for today's students—which generally require spending more money—and preserving and growing capital to maintain the educational experience for future generations. The governing board also owes a duty to previous generations in that the intentions of past donors must be taken into account when determining the appropriate deployment of endowment assets, and they are bound by UPMIFA, which requires the board to preserve intergenerational equity and honor donor intent regarding the preservation of funds.

Target spending rate. In working through the process of setting a target spending rate, three important considerations quickly come to the fore: investment returns, intergenerational equity, and budget impact.

The most obvious factor is the relationship between the spending rate and investment returns. Endowments are expected to support the institution in perpetuity, and the level of support required will grow commensurately with the size of the institution and the cost increases it faces. To maintain the purchasing power of the endowment, it is important that the endowment's long-term expected returns exceed its annual spending rate by a margin that at least offsets inflation. This preserves the corpus of the endowment in real terms. Ideally, incremental endowment returns allow the endowment to grow with the institution.

Most real-return targets are based on the consumer price index (CPI), a broad-based measure of the general price level intended to capture how the cost of the average consumer's basket of goods and services evolves over time. This measure of inflation does not fully capture the price pressures faced by institutions of higher learning, though. The measure of inflation for colleges and universities is called the Higher Education Price Index (HEPI). This measure of inflation is typically significantly higher than the CPI, placing an additional burden on university budgets. This additional cost pressure on university budgets should be taken into account when considering the appropriate investment and spending policies for the institution and should also be considered when setting any management fees to be charged by the institution for the management of the funds taken by the organization.

The better-than-expected investment returns in recent years have facilitated higher contributions from the endowment to support the operating budget. These high returns cannot be counted upon in future, as valuations across a broad range of assets appear stretched. The prospect of a return to more normal levels of asset valuations and returns casts doubt on the sustainability of the current level of increases in support being provided to the budget by the endowment. This is leading more institutions to scrutinize their spending policies. In the following, we consider different approaches to determining spending formulas.

Spending Formulas. Formal spending policies are designed and adopted for many reasons, including guiding the institution's decision-makers and educating its many constituents; preventing ad hoc decision-making; and maintaining predictability and consistency. There remain three major types of spending policies in widespread use: percentage of market value, growth in spending, and a weighted average, which is a mix of the two.

- *Percentage of market value.* This approach calculates the spendable amount as a predetermined percentage (say, 4.5 percent) of the market value of the endowment. The market value is most often calculated over a number of trailing quarters (12 is most common) to smooth out the year-to-year volatility of the amount available for spending. For years, this has been the most common method used by the majority of institutions.

   There are two disadvantages to this approach. First, the amount of the endowment's contribution to the budget can change significantly due to market moves from year to year, notwithstanding attempts at smoothing out variations, thus complicating budgetary management. Second, the availability of abundant resources in good times could loosen the reins of budgetary discipline, leading to unsustainably high outlays that will ultimately require painful retrenchment.

- *Growth in spending.* Another policy used by some institutions targets budgetary contributions in dollar terms, with a constant increase around the level of inflation as measured by the CPI or HEPI, which usually translates to an increase of 2–3 percent from year to year. The main advantage of this policy is its predictability—it sets the dollar amount used from the endowment for budgetary purposes in a way that is independent of the endowment's assets. This predictability is also its main potential disadvantage, as implementing this policy could deplete the endowment in a protracted period of subpar investment returns. Conversely, if the endowment's assets grow particularly rapidly over a sustained period, implementing this rule could artificially constrain the budget by retaining too much money in the endowment.

- *Weighted average.* Most institutions that are changing the methodologies for calculating their spending rates are moving to a weighted average of both approaches, in an effort to dampen the primary disadvantages of each by employing a mix of both. The weighted average is computed by taking a weighted average of prior spending in dollars, (generally given a 60 percent to 80 percent weighting), adjusted for inflation, and the amount that would have been spent using a percentage of current endowment market value (generally given a weighting of 20 percent to 40 percent).[2] The weighted-average approach allows the spending rate to rise as a share of total assets in bad markets, but not by too much. In up markets, spending in dollar terms will increase, but by less than under the percentage-of-market-value approach.

Another approach that improves on the first two adds an alternative rule as a boundary or constraining factor. For example, a percentage-of-market-value spending rule can be modified by the addition of a growth-in-spending constraint as follows: Spend 4.5 percent of the trailing 12-quarter average market value, subject to a minimum increase (over the prior year's spending) equal to 1 percent and a maximum increase of inflation plus 4 percent. The addition of the latter clause ensures that the current year's spending is a reasonable increment over the prior year's spending. Likewise, a pure growth-in-spending rule can be modified as follows: Increase spending by inflation plus 1 percent, subject to a minimum of 3 percent and a maximum of 7 percent of the trailing three-year average market value. The latter qualifier ensures that the actual spending rate does not deviate too far from the targeted rate.

Spending policies, like investment policies, should be reviewed annually, but changed infrequently—and only for compelling reasons other than recent market conditions. An organization should not be looking to change from formula to formula to maximize spending—for example, changing to a weighted-average formula in bad markets (so the spending distribution is a higher dollar level) and to a percentage-of-market-value formula in strong markets (again, so the spending distribution is a higher dollar level). A pattern of tactically tinkering with spending policy, which generally has the effect of maximizing spending, can be a symptom of weak governance.

As illustrated in figure 1.1, the average endowment has had an effective spending rate typically between 4 percent and 5 percent over the past 20 years. There are two variables that contribute to the change in the effective rate, and it is difficult to attribute them without underlying details that comprise the rates used in the charts. The first variable is the nominal percentage used in the spending formula, and as discussed, more institutions are looking to lower the spending rate from 5 percent to something like 4.5 percent. Secondly, there is a reverse relationship in the effective spending rate and the market value. When portfolios are declining in value, the effective spending rate will increase, as you see during the credit crisis in 2008–2009. When portfolios are growing, the effective spending rate declines. The smoothing tactics used in most spending formulas mean that changes phase in gradually.

Figure 1.1 Average Annual Effective Spending Rates* for Total Institution for Fiscal Years 2001–2020

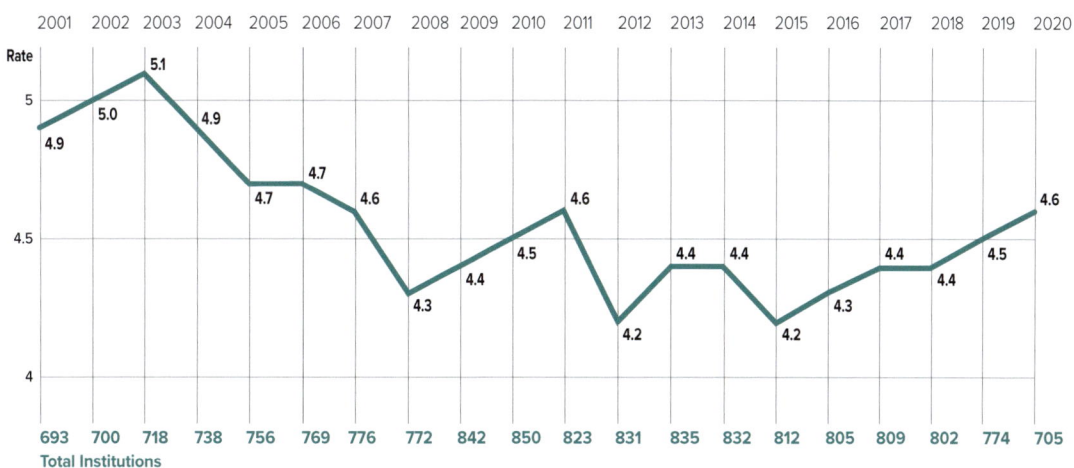

* equal-weighted

Sources: 2010 NACUBO-Commonfund Study of Endowments, *Figure 5.1;* 2015 NACUBO-Commonfund Study of Endowments, *Figure 5.1;* 2020 NACUBO-TIAA Study Of Endowments.

Endowment Composition

Donors and Endowments

What motivates donors to give large sums of money to endow an institution or activity? Why do people give or bequeath endowment funds for specific purposes as opposed to donating money that can be spent at any time for any purpose? Although the reasons may be complex, two generalizations can safely be made.

First, donors often wish to ensure that a given activity will exist in perpetuity. A particular program may already exist, or the gift may provide the impetus for its formation. In either case, the donor of an endowed program generally expects it to survive forever despite institutional change that otherwise might cause a shift in priorities and possible loss of funding. Accepting an endowment gift contractually binds an institution to the priorities specified in the trust agreement.

Institutions should strive to include provisions in their agreements with donors that allow them to reassess an endowment's goals after a specified period of time or should the purposes of the gift become impossible, impracticable, or illegal to fulfill, and, if necessary, redirect the proceeds to an alternative use closely aligned with the donor's original intent. Although colleges and universities may try to change outmoded restrictions by appealing to the donor or the courts, due to legal restrictions, institutions cannot unilaterally change the terms of an endowment gift greater than $25,000 because the gift agreement acts as a legal agreement binding the institution to abide by the terms outlined. (Some state UPMIFA statues enable institutions to change the purposes of funds that have become difficult to expend and that are below a certain threshold value and/or older than a given age.)

A second reason endowments are popular among donors is that some individuals are focused on their legacy. Rare is the university building that does not bear the name of a generous donor who enabled its construction. Balancing the motivations of donors with the needs of the university requires a deft touch.

As a result of the way funds are raised, an endowment is a pooled collection of hundreds or even thousands of individual funds, as well as some unrestricted funds. Most of the individual funds have restrictions set forth by the donor on how the funds will be used. As noted, common uses include student financial aid, faculty support, and research. Unrestricted funds, as the name implies, provide flexibility to the institution on how the funds will be used. For a growing number of schools, these funds provide valuable contributions and diversification to the operating budget.

Building an Endowment

Colleges and universities can build an endowment in two ways: fundraising and generating investment returns greater than the spending rate plus inflation.

Fundraising. The board determines fundraising priorities and building an endowment must be central among them. The board may be constrained by donor preferences, but fundraising efforts should be tailored to prioritize endowment giving, especially unrestricted gifts. There is always a fine balance to be struck between the operational flexibility of unrestricted gifts, the use of which can evolve with the changing needs of the institution, and the interest of donors in restricting gifts to specific, cherished purposes. It is essential to grow endowment assets in a balanced way. No endowment can expect to grow as much as desired by relying on investment returns alone.

Douglas Phillips, the long-standing chief investment officer at the University of Rochester and former treasurer of Williams College, remarked on the importance of fundraising as he accepted the 2010 NACUBO Rodney H. Adams Endowment Management Award, which recognizes excellence in investment leadership at a college or university. Phillips said:

> What interests me about this history is that a large part of the post-WWII alumni support was designated as permanent endowment, which I interpret as a sign of faith in the future of America. But I was also puzzled by the wide variation between schools in the level of support since WWII, particularly in gifts to endowment. This causes enormous differences in endowment growth rates, and consequently the level of support provided to faculty and students. *It turns out that this compounding of giving to endowments is a much more*

important factor in endowment growth than investment performance. So what causes these differences in support? Are alumni of certain schools unhappy with their education? Are schools underinvesting in their advancement and alumni-relations programs? Do certain schools attract and graduate wealthier people? Well, I never did find conclusive answers to these questions, but I am now fairly certain that failed alumni relations and advancement programs have a lot to do with the differences in support. And I am also fairly certain that a good advancement program at a college or university generates gifts that amount to 10 times the cost of running the program.

An important nuance of endowment funding is the use of institutional set-asides, which refer to funds that are not specifically designated by donors for the endowment but are devoted to this use by the governing board. (Nearly all institutional set-asides are designated as *quasi-endowment*, because there are no legal restrictions on the future use of principal.) The two sources of institutional set-asides are *internally generated cash* and *unrestricted gifts* of all types. Internally generated cash typically results from operating surpluses or a buildup of reserves and can be brought into the endowment by board action. Trustees may also direct any unrestricted gifts—including bequests and matured planned gifts (charitable remainder trusts, gift annuities, and pooled income funds)—into the endowment. Such actions should be taken if trustees wish to prioritize endowment growth.

Institutionally Related Foundations

Most public colleges and universities have an affiliated foundation that serves as a gift repository and manages the endowment on behalf of the institution. Institutionally related foundations were created, in part, to segregate privately contributed funds from state money and to avoid the restrictions state entities may be subject to regarding investments and other operations. Affiliated foundations also provide a solution to a governance challenges associated with public higher education. Public colleges' and universities' governing boards are either elected or, more commonly, appointed by the state governor or legislature. Institutions that are part of a system may not have their governing board operating under the oversight of a system board. Public institution governing boards are typically smaller than private institution boards and may be stretched thin giving the scope of their responsibilities and lack the diversity of expertise and perspective essential to effectively managing an endowment.

In contrast, affiliated foundations are set up as private nonprofits. They recruit their own board members and can engage volunteers with the skills, experience, and expertise needed to oversee endowment management. Foundation board members are often recruited from the ranks of the most generous donors to an institution and can represent donor perspectives in investment decision-making. The independent governing boards of foundations can provide oversight and stewardship of privately contributed gifts funds, ensuring that donor intent is honored in regard to both uses of funds and spending rates, and, when necessary, resist short-term pressures from the institution to draw down funds to address current needs at the expense of the long-term purchasing power of the endowment.

In addition to receiving and managing gift funds, foundations often oversee fundraising on behalf of the institution and may accept, acquire, and develop real estate and undertake other work to support the institution. Foundation boards are, for most public institutions, the premier philanthropic leadership body. Foundation board members are typically expected to make annual gifts, at least one major or leadership gift, and are often expected to include the institution in their estate plans. While foundation boards may have a wide range of responsibilities, they can be focusing their attention (and be composed with an eye towards) philanthropic leadership and endowment management. This is a powerful combination. Prospective donors can look at such a board and have confidence that their gifts will be stewarded and invested appropriately when the board and investment committee members overseeing and managing endowments are among the principal donors to the institution.

While the ability to independently fulfill governance responsibilities and serve as stewards of gift funds are important benefits of affiliated foundations, foundation boards, as a function of their foundation's mission, have an obligation to support the mission and priorities of the institution. Foundation investment committees need to work closely with the institution's president or chancellor and chief financial officer to ensure that risk and return parameters, liquidity safeguards, and spending policies are closely aligned with and informed by institutional finances and priorities. They should also provide the institution with regular reports on endowment performance and projected returns and spending distributions.

Finally, foundations typically assess an "endowment management fee" to fund their operations. To the extent that such fees support fundraising operations, they might be considered among the endowment's highest yield and lowest risk investment. Data from the CASE Voluntary Support of Education (VSE) Survey found that in 2018 the return on investment in fundraising was 943% (for 101 institutions of a variety of types). For research/doctoral institutions every ten cents invested in fundraising yielded a dollar of philanthropic support. The longitudinal VSE data also indicates that higher investment in fundraising yields higher returns.

The *AGB Board of Directors' Statement on Institution-Foundation Partnerships* (2016) provides an overview of principles and practices supporting effective collaboration between institutions and affiliated foundations.

In fact, it is good budget discipline to consider establishing a formal policy that all unrestricted bequests and matured planned gifts exceeding a certain amount automatically become part of the endowment, yet we recognize that some organizations have thoughtfully used significant gifts towards compelling institutional transformations which may stimulate additional giving. It would also be worthwhile to consider adding all unrestricted gifts in excess of a certain budgeted amount to the endowment. Since such windfalls typically are not part of the budget process, there is a strong rationale for allowing such funds to become a permanent funding source for the college, rather than being spent immediately. We would encourage institutions looking to grow their endowments to consider implementing such a policy.

Investment returns in excess of spending. Colleges and universities can also build an endowment by generating investment returns in excess of the chosen spending rate. But, as discussed earlier, this is a less reliable strategy in the near term, and we strongly advise against assuming unrealistic rates of return. Generating greater investment returns usually involves a sophisticated approach, building a more diversified and complex portfolio, and potentially incurring greater risks. It is essential to calibrate the expected return and risk characteristics of the endowment portfolio, taking into consideration a realistic assessment of the impact of bad outcomes on the broader finances of the institution. We will explore later in this book some of the main tools used to optimize the balance between investment risk and return.

Fundraising and Endowment Performance

Balancing immediate budgetary pressures with the need for the endowment to grow commensurately with a growing institution is challenging in all market environments. It is especially fraught during periods of market stress. A growing and steady stream of gifts becomes a critical part of the solution to ease these pressures.

Given these pressures, along with the increasing engagement of donors determined to ensure that their gifts will be handled well, investment and development committees—and their staffs—must work in concert. Optimal communication of the investment strategy should not be left solely to the development office. All who govern and lead an institution must be knowledgeable about the investment approach and engaged in communicating with key constituents in order to maximize the strategy's success.

Often, the same interests that compel donors to give large sums to an institution make them demanding judges of how their money is invested and spent. While institutions are justified in seeking to maintain the maximum amount of flexibility in determining how to use gifts, it should be expected that donors will desire some regular insight into the investment process. The last decade has brought about a sharp increase in such activism. A transparent, dynamic, and robust process, whether carried out by an internal or outsourced investment team, may encourage greater generosity on the part of existing and prospective donors. Success breeds success: It is often the case that a well-managed endowment with a strong growth rate will attract more philanthropy than one that has posted weak performance figures, although the latter may have a greater need for new gifts.

Summary

To exercise their fiduciary responsibilities effectively, investment committees supervising the investment and spending policies of endowments should have a good grasp of the institutional and regulatory context in which the endowment operates. The appropriate asset mix for the endowment, its targeted return, and its tolerance for risk all must be guided by a firm understanding of how the endowment fits into the broader mosaic of a college's or university's complex operations and finances. This institutional and regulatory knowledge is an essential building block for assessing the relative merits of the various strategies used to construct a diversified investment portfolio.

We turn in chapter 2 to a consideration of investment governance and, in the chapters that follow, consider the main elements of the design and implementation of an endowment's investment policy.

Key Questions for Boards

1. What steps have we taken to make sure all board members understand the interplay of operational, financial, and investment considerations at the institution?

2. Has the college or university administration done all it can to educate all trustees concerning their fiduciary responsibilities? Do board meetings include regular educational sessions on fiduciary responsibilities; e.g., on an annual basis?

3. What have committee members done to ensure that the size of the endowment, the expected investment returns, and the level of annual spending from the endowment are aligned with the institution's current and future needs and strategic objectives?

4. Does the board support and invest in fundraising and demonstrate philanthropic leadership?

5. What else can the institution do to emphasize building the endowment?

Chapter 2

Best Practices for Successful Endowment Management

Effective governance draws on many interconnected strands, including shared objectives and values, a commitment to high standards, a deeply ingrained code of conduct, well-defined roles and responsibilities, and clear lines of accountability. The fiduciary responsibilities of care, loyalty, and obedience weave together these many strands, nurturing a culture of strong governance that furthers institutional mission and goals.

In this chapter, we consider the critical elements of a robust governance structure for endowment management and offer perspectives on shaping them to successfully guide one of the most significant financial responsibilities of higher education boards.

Recommendations for Building Successful Investment Committees

1. Clearly delineate and document the role and authority of all key parties involved in management of the endowment. Boards, committees, investment staff, and outside advisors can work together in many different ways to accomplish the myriad tasks involved in endowment management. Above all, it is critical that committee members know what is expected of them; this orientation should take place when they are recruited to join the endowment committee. Some committees choose a model in which greater authority is granted to a CIO—either an internal Chief Investment Officer (CIO) or an Outsourced Chief Investment Officer (OCIO)—to take any action that is consistent with the investment policy. Others choose a model in which few investment actions can happen without approval from the investment committee. To avoid confusion, reduce frustration, and make the process efficient, it is imperative to clarify—in writing—the specific tasks, responsibilities, and authority of all parties involved in the endowment-management process. Nothing should be assumed. (A complete description of the various models of endowment management may be found later in this chapter; for the purposes of this section, CIO will denote an internal, outsourced, or committee professional.)

Some colleges and universities include a statement addressing the division of responsibilities in the investment policy, which we recommend later in the book, while for others, it is part of a separate operating policy. Many institutions, however, have no such document. This can often lead to friction among the various parties, who make conflicting assumptions about their own and others' authority and responsibilities. This is likely a leading cause of CIO turnover, which rarely is a positive for endowment performance.

In its fiduciary role, the governing board must always retain some key, high-level endowment-management responsibilities that should be explicitly stated. Today, best practices suggest that these may include:

- Determine the structure and composition of the investment committee (see recommendation #2).
- Select the investment committee chair.
- Approve the endowment-management model (internal CIO, OCIO, committee-led, or something else).
- Establish and monitor the conflict-of-interest policy.
- Approve any DEI- and ESG-related policies and initiatives. (See more on this in chapter 4.)
- Establish guidelines for any major investment policy issue on which the board has strong views (e.g., limits on illiquidity).
- Regularly review the major decisions and performance of the investment committee.

There are two key decisions that are often recommended to the board for final approval, but where all critical work and analysis is performed by the investment committee:

- Selection and termination of the CIO, OCIO, or consultant.
- Approval of the investment policy statement, which should include the strategic asset allocation, allowable asset classes, and approved ranges for each asset class.

To facilitate timely decision-making, there are other decisions that should not require approval by the board. Today, best practices suggest that the investment committee be empowered to perform the following strategic tasks:

- Recommend the endowment-management model to the board.
- Approve any temporary departures from investment policy and communicate this to the board.
- Support the CIO/OCIO/consultant and ensure he or she has sufficient resources.
- Review investment performance compared to appropriate benchmarks.
- Review portfolio exposures and risks.
- Review all major actions taken by the CIO/OCIO/consultant, and his or her performance.
- Review the level of endowment-related fees and expenses.
- Help source managers.
- Communicate with other constituents, including donors, board members, and other committees of the board.
- Approve the independent, third-party custodian of the endowment assets.
- Ensure adherence to all applicable laws, regulations, and policies for the institution, such as UPMIFA, public records laws, etc.

A number of years ago, the institutionally related foundations (IRFs) associated with public universities were not subject to the same open records laws as the public universities they supported. In an increasing number of states, however, these gaps in disclosure and the "sunniness" of the information required has closed. What this means varies by state and it creates complexities for organizations who wish to keep some details of their investment program confidential. They may choose to keep this confidential to honor agreements with managers who do not choose for their return or fee information to be disclosed on websites. Each state is different and trustees should be educated on your state's specific considerations and implications.

Best practices also require that the CIO be delegated—and then be held accountable for—most implementation of day-to-day tasks. These include:

- Developing and drafting the investment policy statement working in close collaboration with the committee.
- Manager sourcing, due diligence, selection, monitoring, and termination.
- Tactical asset allocation within approved asset-allocation ranges.
- Recommending changes to investment policy.
- Managing portfolio exposures and risks, which includes rebalancing.
- Monitoring and reporting on the following to the investment committee:
  - Investment performance
  - Portfolio risks and exposures
  - Compliance with investment policy
  - Endowment-management fees and expenses
  - Legal review and negotiation of contracts.

The role of a consultant, if employed, should also be clearly defined. Institutions use investment consultants in several different ways. For example, the consultant may report to the committee as its independent advisor. He or she may function as the institution's entire investment staff or may report to the CIO or CFO and serve as an extension of staff. Though rare, some will be delegated limited discretion.

Different institutions are free to adjust the above roles and responsibilities to meet their specific needs. The key, however, is to clarify—in writing—the specific authority and responsibilities of all parties involved. Doing so will avoid confusion, reduce frustration, and increase the efficiency and effectiveness of the endowment-management process.

2. Consciously shape the committee's composition. Selecting members of the investment committee is a crucial task that requires a thorough assessment of his or her ability to contribute to the work of the committee, commitment to the institution, and willingness to take on a significant governance role in protecting the financial future of the institution. He or she should also have the ability to work in a collegial manner with other committee members and possess the disposition

to respect the roles and responsibilities of other parties. Nearly every organization has experienced difficult behavior on the part of a committee member—perhaps a major donor—who has asserted inappropriate influence.

Colleges and universities can improve their chances of building a value-adding committee by seeking to add two specific types of individuals: chief investment officers from other nonprofits and noninvestment professionals with good common sense and sound judgment.

Those who serve or have served successfully as chief investment officers at other endowments and foundations bring great advantages as committee members that others simply cannot duplicate for many reasons, including their accumulated relevant knowledge and experience. They possess a deep understanding of the trade-offs of various asset allocations as well as the advantages, disadvantages, and cycles of asset classes. CIOs and ex-CIOs are usually experienced in sourcing, analyzing, and recruiting top money managers. They understand what it takes to be successful and are aware of the pitfalls to avoid. CIOs who have previously dealt with consultants, money managers, and investment committees will typically enjoy a valuable, measured, and firsthand perspective on attracting, retaining, and overseeing the CIO—whether external or internal. This responsibility can be the investment committee's single most important contribution to successful endowment management.

Other individuals with a strong likelihood of being excellent investment committee members are noninvestment professionals with good common sense. Of course, it helps if they have some general knowledge of investing so that they do not get lost in detailed discussions. Such individuals bring the valuable and broader perspective of one who is not actively involved in the markets. Interestingly, noninvestment professionals are more likely to question assumptions that investment professionals take for granted. They also are generally more willing to delegate appropriate implementation authority.

It is commonly believed that money-management executives make good committee members. This conventional wisdom is often—though not always—misguided for several reasons. First, money managers are extremely knowledgeable about their particular sectors, but rarely understand other asset classes or the management of a multiasset class portfolio. Second, money managers are programmed to take action on a daily basis and as a result, their horizons are often shortened. In their world, every day brings a news flow that could be acted upon immediately. Successful endowment oversight is, in some respects, the polar opposite—maintaining a long-term investment policy despite the news of the day. Managers should not be encouraged to take frequent actions based on the market, economic, political, or other news of the day. Finally, money managers often have a strong bias toward their particular areas of expertise, at times pitting their sector against other sectors. For all these reasons, college and university boards should be absolutely convinced that a money manager can make the mental switch from active manager to patient committee member before offering him or her a seat on the committee.

Three character traits should be actively sought in all prospective investment committee members: patience, a willingness to listen to others, and a sense of humility. The most dangerous committee members are overconfident and impatient individuals who think that they can lead the committee to outsmart the market. Such individuals are susceptible to promoting actions that detract from performance, including return chasing, market timing, frequent asset allocation changes, and high levels of manager churning. They may also be dismissive of other committee members.

In addition to a diversity of professional skills to foster optimal decision-making, it is important to include cultural, ethnic and gender diversity to ensure that the management of the endowment has the benefit of a range of perspectives. There is a growing body of research showing that diverse groups make more informed decisions and often achieve better results. McKinsey & Company, a highly regarded management-consulting organization, found that gender diversity on boards correlates with "significantly higher earnings and returns on equity." Moreover, investment committees should be diverse in terms of the ages of members to ensure stability and continuity and to provide the perspectives of different generations. Finally, differences in socioeconomic backgrounds are important

For those institutions that break out finance and investments into two separate committees, institutions have found it helpful to have some overlap between them as well as some members who have been on the board for long periods of time and possess a solid understanding of the whole institution. These things lead to a better understanding of how the endowment fits into the broader finances of the institution.

3. Consider inviting nonboard members to serve on the committee. This can be a good way to: 1) acquire some of the professional skills needed to round out a committee, without asking someone to commit to the board; 2) cultivate prospective board members by bringing them on board for a more focused task first; and 3) reengage board members whose terms have expired. In all cases, committee members must be fully committed to the institution and understand how the portfolio fits into the broader financial picture of the institution and supports the mission. Including committee members with little or no affiliation with the board or the institution may be a wonderful way to engage talent, but it is ultimately most important that all committee members be prepared for the hard work of being effective fiduciaries. This commitment often requires some deep emotional connection to the organization served.

Optimizing the Selection of Investment Committee Members

By Nikki Kraus and Ken Grossfield, Strategic Investment Group

Optimizing the selection of investment committee members is a crucial task that greatly contributes to endowment management success. To help committees make appropriate decisions beyond "time, talent, and treasure" considerations, we developed a grid of skills and attributes to help identify individuals for inclusion on a committee, which is a constructive way to guide thinking about maximizing the effectiveness of this group of five to eight members.

As you view the grid, please keep in mind:

1. Personality attributes are as important as subject matter expertise.

2. Seek to add two specific types of individuals: chief investment officers from similar institutions as well as non-investment professionals with good common sense and sound judgment.

3. Money management professionals are not always good committee members.

   While there is a benefit to having members with in-depth knowledge of certain asset classes, particularly alternative investments, there are some issues to consider. Money managers can be knowledgeable about their particular sectors, but may rarely think about risk/return tradeoffs associated with multi-asset class portfolios. There may also be a horizon mismatch between their day jobs (short) and endowments (long). Their work may also require great conviction and decisive action, which may not serve the more collaborative and inclusive nature of a well-functioning committee.

4. The most dangerous committee members are overconfident and impatient individuals who want to pursue market timing strategies and feel their voices are more valuable than others'.

   Committee members who are overconfident or impatient may undermine the deliberations of the committee.

5. Promote diversity.

6. Don't consider "treasure" alone when asking people to serve.

   Time and talent contributions, in the right balance, can help an endowment committee achieve critical educational mission objectives.

Investment Committee Member Matrix of Skills

Personality Attributes/ Skills	Required	Great to Have	Not Needed	Never Needed
Love of institution	All			
Asks big picture questions	At least one			
Reluctant to speak up even when they disagree				X
Speaks over others and demands their proposed action be taken				X
Willingness to listen to others' opinions, especially when different from theirs	All			
Commitment to do required work of committee	All			
Tenure on committee greater than 10 years to provide institutional memory	At least one			
Tenure on committee less than 3 years to promote new ideas	At least one			
CIO experience		At least one		
Attorney		At least one		
CEO / Senior business leader		At least one		
General money management executive			X	
Alternative investment experience		At least one		
Diversity by gender, ethnicity, full scholarship kids / full pay kids		At least one of each		

AGB.org Blog, October 23, 2018

4. Choose the chair of the committee carefully. A proficient chair is essential to an effective investment committee, and the president and chair of the full board should be certain that the leader of the investment committee is carefully chosen. He or she should be an experienced investment professional or veteran committee chair who possesses a strong knowledge of institutional investing while fully understanding the committee's charge. It is impossible to overstate the importance of this critical role: it can mean the difference between excellence and mediocrity. The chair should also not be new to the committee in order to maintain stability in the approach, a key determinant to success. A successful committee chair must be able to:

a. *Work closely with the president and board chair to recruit and support effective committee members.*

b. *Manage a committee member who attempts to assert greater influence than is appropriate.* No committee member can make a gift large enough to compensate for the potential damage he or she might do to the endowment's value.

c. *Maintain a culture of collegiality and respect.* An open and honest exchange of views in which all perspectives are carefully weighed is critical to sound decision-making and is a key attribute of effective committees.

5. Limit the size of the committee. Committees need to be appropriately sized. They should be of sufficient size to shoulder the work of the committee and to allow for a diversity of perspectives yet be small enough to be productive and encourage meaningful individual involvement. Investment committees in particular benefit from being small. The inherent difficulties of committee decision-making compound with size. Furthermore, consensus decisions in the investment world—unlike other areas of life—are likely to be poor decisions. The best decisions tend to be contrarian ones. Large (and short-tenured) committees can be an obstacle to acting on contrarian investment ideas. The more involved a committee gets in implementation, the smaller it needs to be.

Most experienced practitioners agree that small investment committees are more effective. Limiting the committee to five to eight individuals will produce a group better able to stay focused on the tasks at hand (setting investment policy and monitoring performance), reach decisions in a timely manner, and work most constructively among themselves and with the CIO. Too often, however, institutions yield to the pressure of large donors and others who wish to be named to the committee and end up with groups larger than optimal.

6. Preserve institutional memory. Proper committee structure should seek an appropriate balance in time served by its members. Investment committees on which the average tenure of members is short, turnover is high, and institutional memory is lost are unlikely to be effective. Stability in membership is extremely important. On the other hand, a modest level of regular turnover is desirable in order to bring fresh ideas, new energy, and different perspectives to the committee.

Given the unique nature of many institutions, we recognize that there are various ways organizations can structure their board and committee membership to achieve these objectives. Some institutions seek to achieve these objectives through term limits. Many feel that properly structured term limits will ensure consistency of membership, but also secure a gradual and orderly transition to new members. While it can be difficult to find good investment committee members, term limits can be desirable because they:

- Protect the committee against stagnation.
- Help attract busy or high-quality members who may be more willing to commit to a finite term.
- Provide the committee with new members who are more likely to question the status quo.
- End the life-membership mentality possessed by some who see their permanent involvement as a right earned through generous financial support.
- Serve as an effective way to deal with unproductive or troublesome members.

Two or three terms of three-to-five years each often works nicely. Terms should be staggered to avoid the departure of several members, especially long-serving ones, at the same time. A steady, but gradual, turnover in committee membership will support the development of good chemistry and preserve institutional memory while allowing for the injection of fresh thinking.

There are shortcomings to term limits because they may carry the risk of avoiding timely confrontation with a poorly behaving member of the committee (while simply waiting for his or her term to end). Terming out also includes the possibility of losing a productive member of the board who could still greatly contribute to the success of the institution, a situation that some suggest may be resolved by granting term exceptions for special people. We would suggest that creates another set of issues; full board decisions about structuring term limits are more feasible or, as AGB has advocated, the practice of regular self-assessments by the board can be an effective means of ensuring self-examination and shared responsibility. Finally, succession planning is critical to long-term success.

7. Ensure open and regular communication with other key members of the institution—especially the finance committee and the full board. Important stakeholders should be kept abreast of the investment committee's work, the committee's results, and any major changes that are taking place. A concise executive summary (two pages should suffice) that contains long-term endowment performance against relevant benchmarks, actual asset allocation vs. the policy, and key decisions recently made should be included in every board meeting package. We also recommend regular in-person updates for the full board, which tends to instill greater levels of trust and confidence in the team that manages the endowment. Nothing replaces face-to-face conversations and the opportunity for board members to ask questions.

Investment Committee Succession Planning

By Nikki Kraus and Tim O'Hara, Strategic Investment Group

Every investment committee should have a succession plan with three primary goals: preserving institutional memory, finding the best committee leadership, and welcoming new ideas.

Preserving Institutional Memory: The ideal average tenure of committee members is 6–7 years, but exceptionally qualified members should be encouraged to remain longer. There is a correlation between average tenure and the committee's time horizon when making investment decisions. It is troubling that so many investment committees no longer have a single member who served during the financial crisis of 2008–2009.

It is advisable that some investment committee members have previous experience on the finance committee, to ensure that they have a broader understanding of the organization's economic situation.

The investment committee should never be the first assignment of a new board member. An investment committee member with no other experience on the board may be inclined to take too much or too little risk with the portfolio.

Term limits should be staggered to avoid the simultaneous departure of several members, especially long-serving ones. There should be exceptions to term limits under certain circumstances, such as when you have a brilliant, very dedicated member with a great institutional history. The automatic removal of several key members at the same time undermines stability, a key component of committee and investment success.

Optimizing Leadership: The committee chair should always be the best-qualified member, not merely the largest donor or the member with the longest service. No committee member can make a gift large enough to compensate for the potential damage he or she might do to the endowment's value. The chair must also be able to maintain a culture of collegiality and respect. An open and honest exchange of views in which all perspectives are carefully weighed—including the ideas of new members—is crucial to sound decision making. And the chair must be strong enough to restrain a member who attempts to exert greater influence than is appropriate.

The chair should never be new to the committee, and to ensure stability would ideally have served as vice chair the year before. An inexperienced chair may not understand why certain past decisions were made, and thus insist on potentially costly changes.

New Ideas: It is crucial to balance stability and openness to new ideas. Stagnation is as much of a danger as sudden change. A well-crafted succession plan can help achieve that balance.

Diversity is key. Members of different ages, genders, races, identities, and socioeconomic backgrounds can bring valuable and important insights and perspectives. Committees have as much to learn from alumni who enjoyed full scholarships as they do from those who paid full price (not to mention those who incurred debt along the way). The committee should be as varied as the student body itself, and should attempt to recruit younger members to help ensure the institution's future.

A thoughtful succession plan is both a look into the future and a nod toward the past. Change is inevitable—though sometimes uncomfortable—and careful planning is necessary to ensure stability and avoid chaos.

AGB.org Blog, December 13, 2018

8. Examine thyself. This is an important part of what AGB recommends to all boards, and we encourage this step at the committee level to facilitate successful operations. Some topics for self-evaluation and related questions include:

a. *Mission awareness.* Does the committee have a clearly articulated and shared understanding of the endowment's investment objectives and constraints?

b. *Governance structure.* Does the committee have a clear understanding of its roles and responsibilities? Are they appropriate? Does the committee spend most of its time on the most important issues? Is there an optimal number of members?

c. *Decision-making process.* Has the committee made wise and timely decisions? In the long term, this can be determined by comparing the endowment's investment performance to appropriate benchmarks. What does the committee do well? What has gone wrong? How could the process be improved?

d. *Attitudes and biases.* Does the committee have any biases that are impacting its decision-making? Does it carefully examine the reports, analyses, and recommendations it receives?

e. *Controls.* Has the committee established clear financial, risk-management, and other controls to ensure the fulfillment of its fiduciary responsibilities?

9. Require an orientation for each new committee member. As new members are brought onto the investment committee, the CIO (if applicable), committee chair, and other staff who support the committee should provide them with a formal orientation before their first meeting. Orientation should include a discussion of the committee's charter, an overview of their fiduciary responsibilities, the conflict-of-interest policy, and a brief summary of current financial and investment issues. Even an experienced investment professional will be unfamiliar with the workings of a particular governing board and its committees. An effective orientation helps ensure that a new member will discharge his or her fiduciary duties with an appropriate working knowledge of the finances of the institution. New members should also be provided with written materials, including:

- The current investment policy statement, with a focus on the official roles and responsibilities of the board, committee, CIO, and advisor.
- Investment committee reports and minutes from the past five years.
- The past three or four executive summaries provided to the board.
- An overview of the institution's financials, including size of the operating budget, composition of the operating budget mix, outstanding debt, enrollment trends, tuition-discounting trends, fundraising levels over time, and major anticipated capital projects.
- Any other significant events in the institution's history or plans for the future.

10. The investment committee of any institution should meet regularly, which we define as at least three times a year in person. In addition, two to three supplemental "check-in" conference calls may be held. During the pandemic, it was not possible to be together in person. Although we may ultimately settle into a schedule that permits one meeting a year to be virtual with little negative effect on the effectiveness of the committee, many committees recognize that the trust, respect and the highest quality decisions are fostered through in-person meetings. We have seen many institutions cut back on the number of meetings, often when markets have delivered strong returns, with the inevitable result that poor endowment performance is blamed on lack of engagement.

11. Members should be prepared to attend all meetings. While it may be impractical, if not impossible, to expect committee members to attend all meetings, the implication is that missing a committee meeting can have consequences for the performance of the committee. If a committee member misses many meetings, productive time will be lost and decision making is impaired. If a member misses the discussion of a new investment, for example, it becomes all too easy for the member to abandon that investment during periods of underperformance. In addition, especially in the early years of working together, it is important that members attend most meetings in person rather than by phone. This helps committee members develop chemistry, thereby boosting trust and confidence within the group. Calling in should be seen as a contingency reserved for exceptional situations. An exception might also be made for a valuable contributor who may live far from campus.

Board Meeting Management Portals

Now more than ever, meeting virtually is critical for governing boards and committees. A number of board meeting portals have sprung up to help fill this gap.

AGB offers a board meeting management platform specifically designed for higher education boards called **AGB OnBoard** (agb.org/onboard/) that provides subscribers a safe and secure digital portal to prepare, organize, and run meetings in real time—for better efficiency and collaboration. AGB OnBoard combines industry-leading board management technology with AGB's resources, insights, and expertise. Key features include:

Proprietary AGB content—*Effective Committee Series* booklets, AGB Board of Directors' Statements, and other books on topics essential to effective board governance

Voting and approval capabilities from any device—allow for trustees and leadership to organize, track, review, comment, and approve decisions digitally

Engagement analytics—record when board book materials are read, where annotations are made, and the agenda sections getting the most attention

E-signatures—keep signed documents and legal agreements organized with other board work

Single sign-on

Zoom video meeting integration

Minutes builder

Industry-leading security and data-protection features

12. If guests are permitted to attend committee meetings, the chair must be firm on their role (as observers) and limit interruptions. If not managed well, the attendance of noncommittee members—who may require background information and additional explanations—will reduce the already limited amount of time available for conducting the committee's business. A meeting should be a working session rather than a public presentation. Certain public institutions may have open-meetings requirements that make enforcement of a "no guest" rule difficult, but every effort should be made to optimize the limited in-person time the committee members have together. Most institutional board members have free time during board meetings and may attend other committee meetings during this time. If that is the case, it is prudent to establish an understanding that all guests are "observers" who should not inject themselves into committee discussion. If the endowment is of critical importance to the entire board—as it is at most institutions—we suggest that boards schedule a brief investment committee update or report at each board meeting. The committee chair should also offer to speak one-on-one with any stakeholder who has questions or would like to learn more.

13. Everyone should be prepared for active participation in committee deliberations. Most committee members are busy professionals with many conflicting commitments. However, it is important that members study materials ahead of time and digest the important information. Meeting materials, including the presentations that will be reviewed and detailed minutes from the prior meeting, should be delivered at least one week in advance. The preparer of these materials should resist the unfortunate and all too common practice of providing briefing books so large that members cannot possibly read and absorb the material.

Concise executive summaries are always welcomed by busy committee members. These can be followed by more detailed information for the few who have the time and inclination to dive into the details. A memo should be enclosed that outlines the key items for discussion, including strategic questions that members need to consider in advance. These measures will allow each member to be an informed participant and help preserve one of the committee's most precious and limited resources—time for robust discussions on strategic items.

Establishing a secure website storing key documents and reports can be an effective tool to help committee members prepare for meetings and provide them with all relevant information without the inconvenience of being weighed down by huge committee packets every quarter. Examples of items to include on the secure website include:

- The investment policy statement
- Executive summaries provided to the board
- Investment managers' fact sheets or executive summaries
- Historical reports on asset allocation and investment performance
- Meeting minutes for the last five years
- Annual fee and expense summaries

Be aware, however, that some committee members prefer good old-fashioned hard copies of meeting materials that they can physically hold and read.

14. Keep comprehensive minutes to document the proceedings and help the committee recall the context surrounding key decisions from meeting to meeting. Continuity demands maintaining informative minutes that include much more than simply actions taken or decisions reached. The specific rationale for major decisions should also be recorded. Committee members should not be expected to recollect why past decisions were made. Detailed minutes assist members in fulfilling their fiduciary duties to monitor the results of prior decisions. Better context should lead to better decisions. For best results, provide the draft minutes to committee members within one week of the meeting, when memories are fresh.

AGB Consulting provides independent board-focused advisory services and can help college, university, and affiliated foundation boards strengthen financial and investment governance practice including board and committee structure and composition, board diversity, board and investment policies, fiduciary responsibilities, and management of potential conflicts of interest. AGB Consulting can also support boards in assessment of investment models and assessment and hiring processes for investment managers and OCIOs. Contact consulting@agb.org for additional information.

Models of Endowment Management

Every institution has someone functioning as chief investment officer, responsible for the many tasks required to implement the investment policy. There are four prevalent models of endowment management, depending on who fills this crucial role:

- Outsourced CIO
- The chair of the committee
- The committee itself, often with the assistance of a consultant
- Internal CIO

Outsourcing the CIO provides an excellent alternative for institutions that do not wish to build their own internal investment office.

1. Outsourced CIO. The use of outside OCIOs has been gathering momentum over the past decade. Institutions with assets ranging from tens of millions to several billions of dollars have engaged an outside fiduciary partner for the management of their portfolios. An outsourced CIO has prescribed discretion to take actions consistent with the investment policy. Unlike a consultant, an outsourced CIO is a decision-maker rather than an advice provider. Implementing active asset allocation tilts, rebalancing, hiring and firing managers, and other day-to-day decisions are delegated by the investment committee to an outside firm functioning as CIO. Most OCIO firms have also built a depth of resources across all aspects of investment management, from front to back office, that is difficult to replicate within an institution—especially those smaller than tens of billions of dollars.

OCIOs benefit from economies of scale in achieving access to top managers and negotiating fees, and potentially enhance performance by bringing more resources to bear on research and portfolio management. Outsourcing can provide a broader range and depth of investment talent than might reasonably be assembled in-house.

In addition to top-tier investment talent and a disciplined investment process, an OCIO can and should provide a wide range of middle- and back-office support. The legal and reporting requirements for an endowment are many and complex and an OCIO can relieve an institution of these burdens.

Although over longer periods of time, the largest endowments (over $1 billion) with sizable internal teams have outperformed smaller endowments by over 1 percent, many investment committees may make an overly simplistic assumption that the model of an internal team is superior to other options. However, successful implementation of an investment program requires an excellent team, and assembling one is anything but easy. It also requires a well-functioning committee. The best practices for governance that we discuss throughout this chapter help a CIO-led program achieve success. Unfortunately, there are plenty of examples of bad governance structures or poorly behaving committees that have led to poor investment results, even when there is an excellent investment team in place.

It should be noted that hiring an OCIO does not signal an end to the committee's responsibilities. The investment committee retains fiduciary responsibility for the most important strategic decisions affecting future performance, including setting the investment strategy and asset allocation, approving the investment policy statement, and providing proper oversight.

This model has several variations depending on the amount of discretion granted to the OCIO and the level of staff involvement. In some discretionary relationships, the OCIO has full authority to hire and fire managers and adjust tactical allocations within the asset class ranges approved by the investment committee. In other cases, the OCIO must first seek approval from the committee.

There are also wide variations within the level of customization offered by OCIOs. At one end of the spectrum, OCIOs may develop and implement a customized portfolio for each client, guided by return objectives, tolerance for risk, liquidity needs, and other pertinent factors. Other OCIOs use a single-fund solution. This less-versatile approach utilizes the OCIO's own commingled, multi-asset class fund in which the assets are managed by outside investment managers to accomplish implementation. Such funds typically reflect the investment strategy and asset allocation of top endowments and foundations, which must be acceptable to the hiring institution. There has been growth of an option in the middle which blends the best thinking of an investment firm with options for customization where appropriate given the institution's needs.

The most obvious problem with OCIOs is the difficulty in hiring and firing them. Committees have a long history of regularly hiring managers near the top of a good performance cycle and then firing them near the bottom of a cycle. How do you prevent committees doing the same with an OCIO? There are no easy answers to this question. In some instances, committees find a search firm to be helpful in navigating the complexities of this important search. Among other things, committees should seek a firm that has the strongest team with relevant experience. The OCIO firm should have a well-reasoned investment process that is judged by the investment committee to have the ability to achieve solid risk-adjusted value added in a manner that is well-aligned with the committee's investment philosophy. Ultimately, the investment committee must reach a judgment on which OCIO is best equipped to achieve the institution's investment objectives, observe its risk limits, and further its mission. Committees should also ask what happens in transition: Do you fire all existing managers or keep some or all of them? What will you hold when you make the switch (commingled funds put together by the OCIO, proprietary products, or separate accounts) and are the holdings portable if the OCIO is relieved of its duties? When reviewing performance, the committee should focus on actual client results where the firm has discretion and seek as much transparency on fees as you can obtain.

2. Committee chair as CIO. For some institutions, having the investment committee chair function as the CIO can be an attractive option—but only if he or she has the right experience. The ideal person to fill this role is a successful CIO (or ex-CIO) from another institution who can utilize the policies, practices, efforts, and resources from his or her day job to benefit the second institution. This approach has been successfully employed at a number of smaller colleges and universities where they are fortunate to have a committee who has the ability to dedicate significant time to the oversight and management of the portfolio.

3. The investment committee functions as the CIO, often with the help of a consultant. We strongly advise against this option. Committees can be very good at establishing policy, but rarely do they have the time, energy, or experience to effectively implement policies. Many investment committees have struggled with implementation while functioning as the CIO. We now have decades of strong evidence that investment committees simply have found it difficult to succeed in this role. There are several obstacles to success:

- *Lack of expertise.* Most committee members, though well intentioned, do not have the education, professional work experience, resources, and/or time to properly plan and implement an investment program.
- *Difficulty in making timely decisions.* Some decisions can't wait until the next quarterly meeting.

- *Inability to make difficult, contrarian decisions, which are likely to be the most profitable.* By definition, a decision reached by consensus of a large committee cannot be contrarian.
- *Diffusion of responsibility.* Someone needs to be held accountable for the success (or failure) of policy implementation. When a committee is in charge, no one is held responsible or accountable.

4. Internal CIO. Effectively performing the role of CIO is a difficult job requiring special expertise and full-time engagement. For this reason, many large and successful institutions have hired an internal CIO. A top-tier investment office may produce millions, even billions, of dollars in incremental growth to an endowment. Creation of an investment office led by a competent CIO should result in a stronger, more advanced investment policy; better implementation of that policy; early adoption of new asset classes and investment strategies; greater due diligence and monitoring of investments; and better decision making. But assembling—and retaining—an excellent team is no easy task. Many institutions have experienced high turnover at the internal CIO level for a number of reasons.

Frequent CIO turnover is disruptive. Investment processes and other personnel almost always change to some degree with each new CIO, and that means costly adjustments in asset allocation, investment philosophy, personnel, management style, and external investment managers, which often have a negative effect on at least shorter-term performance results.

The endowment size at which an institution should build an internal staff is a matter of vigorous debate and for a number of years, many thought this was $1 billion, yet given the increased expertise, systems, and legal work needed to manage a complex portfolio, many believe this has increased to $2 billion or maybe even larger depending on a variety of factors, including the location of an institution. Location has contributed to a greater number of investment offices moving off campus to the nearest big city, in order to retain talent and make it easier for them to engage with managers. Clearly, as the fund size increases, the economics of internal management become more attractive. With an internal team the committee may be able to maintain more direct control and oversight over investment policy decisions, compensation, costs, and fees. However, many institutions, even those with large endowments, allocate surprisingly few resources to establishing and maintaining an internal investment office. To them we offer this bit of advice: **The only thing more expensive than good investment management is lousy investment management.**

The personnel costs, systems, and ancillary expenses of an investment office can be significant, and as a result, some offices are under-resourced, making it difficult for them to achieve the desired results. A CIO must have access to sufficient investment staff and other resources necessary to successfully perform his or her job. The level of resources must be consistent with the size and complexity of the endowment. Trying to develop a sophisticated investment program with a little staff and meager resources will cause problems and may ultimately lead to subpar performance.

Finally, there has been growth in a hybrid model of internal staff that oversee an OCIO who is used to extend internal resources.

Two serious problems that often arise in each of the above models are the lack of clarity about authority and accountability for decisions (which means they can change over time unexpectedly) and the failure of the committee to delegate sufficient implementation authority and responsibility to the CIO. Decision-making typically leads to turf wars and disgruntlement, which contribute to high turnover of staff/outside partners (OCIOs, consultants, and/or managers), and, ultimately, poor performance.

For institutions without an internal or external CIO, a stimulating agenda item for your next investment committee meeting is: our chief investment officer. Questions for discussion include:

- Who is currently functioning as CIO?
- Is this working?
- If we are dissatisfied, what are our options?
- Can we afford *not* to hire a CIO (internal or external)?
- Should we consider outsourcing?

As mentioned previously, there is a growing number of experienced, objective investment professionals who can be retained to help the committee through this exercise.

Whichever model the institution ultimately selects, each party's key roles, responsibilities, and scope of authority must be clearly articulated in writing and agreed upon. This will facilitate more effective working relationships and maximize the probability of success.

Finally, an environment of regular review is critical to optimizing your program. Sit down with your CIO, whether internal or external, formally at least once each year and share a written formal review of what you expected and how they performed based on these expectations. It is especially important to voice concerns and share preferences early. Doing so will give the CIO an opportunity to respond either with corrective action or an explanation.

Many institutions seek help in determining which endowment-management structure will work best for them. We discuss this further in chapter 6.

Common Investment Mistakes

We have observed with regrettable regularity a number of common missteps by investment committees in the management of their endowments that contribute to subpar performance. The most significant recurring mistakes include the following:

Mistake #1: Chasing returns. Chasing performance is *arguably the single largest source of underperformance by investors*. It is a problem that is widely recognized, but rarely avoided. In most areas of business and life, the wise course of action is to do more of what has recently succeeded and avoid that which has failed. In the investment world, however, this modus operandi can be costly. For example, investment committees tend to hire managers after a period of impressive outperformance, then fire them after a period of underperformance. Regularly repeating this pattern produces subpar performance.

Subsidiary Corporation for Managing the Endowment

Some larger institutions rely upon a subsidiary investment-management entity to manage the endowment assets. Among the advantages of this approach are:

1. The ability to pay appropriate investment-related compensation without being subject to the same scrutiny as if they were on the "books" of the college or university.

2. The benefits of separating revenue streams that would count as unrelated business taxable income (UBTI).

3. The ability to recruit members who might not be a good fit for a university board.

4. The opportunity for the CIO to take the helm as CEO and manage the investment operation with the oversight of a board dedicated solely to the function of overseeing the investments.

5. The potential freedom to manage additional outside capital from other institutions in exchange for valuable fee revenue.

6. The ability to free up institution or foundation boards to devote more time to other pressing issues and/or fundraising.

"Groupthink" contributes to the natural human tendency to chase performance. Successful investing, however, often requires the exact opposite—investing in an asset class after a period of severe decline and reducing exposure when an asset class has appreciated strongly. Not following the crowd chasing returns takes fortitude and a strong focus on valuations and long-term results, rather than following fads and bandwagons.

Three key practices will help avoid this pitfall: 1) Strictly adhere to the investment policy, especially in the area of rebalancing; 2) Delegate implementation authority to a contrarian-minded CIO, committee chair, or OCIO; and 3) Ask whether a proposed action would have been a great decision three years ago. A "yes" answer means that the decision is certainly not timely and may be a textbook example of chasing recent performance.

Mistake #2: Misusing peer comparisons. Investors are often influenced by the practices of other institutions, failing to recognize that these institutions may have different circumstances, capabilities, prospects, resources, and strategic goals. We recommend instead that institutions design their investment policies based on a thoughtful and pragmatic understanding of their specific situation and ability to take various forms of risk. At the same time, endowment managers should be aware of what peers are doing in order to learn from them. Any college or university that underperforms its peers long enough or by a wide enough margin—especially when there is a high level of turnover on the investment committee—will certainly hear from donors, and will feel pressure to change the investment strategy, often at the wrong time, in order to avoid finding itself in a weaker competitive position. While such comparisons are natural, it is important to avoid drawing strong conclusions from merely comparing returns. An institution may have generated high returns over a certain period by taking large risks. Alternatively, the peer portfolio may have high returns because of concentrated exposures that were especially favored during the period reported.

Mistake #3: Failing to rigorously analyze the performance track records of managers, the CIO, or the committee itself. Too often institutions uncritically accept flattering representations of performance without analyzing its key drivers and reaching a well-founded expectation for the future prospects of adding value. Investors should probe deeply to gain a long-term perspective of actual performance and the factors driving both strong and subpar returns across market cycles. This analysis helps provide a sense of the investment professional's ability to deliver consistent returns and to predict performance over the course of a cycle. For example, if the long-term results are driven by one strong year's returns, dig deeper: What happened in that year, and what drove returns? Were they the result of one big bet or a number of smaller decisions? Getting one major decision correct is only proof of luck. Getting many decisions correct over multiple years suggests skill and a greater probability of success in the future. Also, read the footnotes associated with performance information. The words "model," "simulated," "hypothetical," or "back-tested" do not represent actual client returns. Healthy skepticism is advised. Seeking the CFA Institute's Global Investment Performance Standards verification provides some assurance that the results were compiled in an appropriate way.

Mistake #4: Taking too much or too little risk. Endowments have long-term horizons that should be used to their advantage when structuring their investment portfolios. Committees may wisely adopt investment policies to achieve a higher level of returns over a long-term horizon, including the ability to deploy an appropriate level of capital into illiquid investments (i.e., private markets), which can be expected to provide higher returns to investors for bearing these risks. However, we have seen numerous examples of committees taking on more risk than they could tolerate and unwinding them at the wrong time. This happens because committees often assume they can endure the impact of these elevated levels of volatility during periods of poor market conditions more than is actually the case, which often leads to abandoning a strategy at just the wrong time.

Other institutions may face the opposite problem. The natural tendency of committee members to avoid negative results during their tenure may unwittingly pressure them to shorten their time horizons and take too little risk. Taking too little risk generally means that the endowment's performance targets will suffer, potentially falling short of its financial objective (inflation plus spending rate) and its peers.

Internalizing the institution's long-term time horizon, understanding its benefits, suppressing one's own individual and shorter time horizon, and preserving the institutional memory of the committee will help the committee to settle on an appropriate level of risk and avoid the costly mistakes of taking on too much or too little risk.

Mistake #5: Misplaced faith in market timing. Another form of hubris common to investors is overconfidence in their ability to time markets, leading to a misuse of tactical moves to add value. Unfortunately, such moves are rarely successful and typically result in poor performance. Serious market timing mistakes have the ability to cripple an endowment for decades. Committees are better served by abandoning their market-timing efforts and, instead, focusing their time and energy on establishing, implementing, and adhering to a well-crafted investment policy designed to achieve better long-term, risk-adjusted returns.

Mistake #6: Failing to maintain a focus on the very long horizon of endowment investing. Committee members may have personal investment horizons of 10 to 20 years while an endowment has an horizon of many times that, and interestingly, many investment committee members associate their term, which may be 3- or 6-years, with the horizon of the endowment. Few want to exit a committee of an organization they care deeply about with a "scorecard" that shows underperformance. Making decisions with a 3-year horizon often does not make sense in the long-term context of endowment funds. Similarly focusing too much attention on short-term fluctuations that are insignificant in the big picture rather than focusing on the long-term return drivers.

For a more detailed look at building strong and successful investment committees, see *The Investment Committee* (AGB, 2011), part of AGB's *Effective Committee Series*.

Summary

Establishing a robust structure of clearly defined roles, responsibilities, and accountability while fostering a culture of good governance is vital to an endowment's long-term success. Promoting favorable chemistry and dynamics within the committee requires strong, judicious leadership and continuous effort that includes periodic self-assessment by the committee. A helpful self-assessment tool can be found in Appendix A. The combination of these efforts is rewarded by a well-informed, patient decision-making structure that can take advantage of the benefits of the long-term horizon of the endowment.

Key Questions for Boards

1. What else should committee members be doing to build a robust investment committee structure that remains effective in the current circumstances?
2. How can the committee continuously foster behaviors to create a culture of best practices?
3. Has the committee established guidelines regarding how often it evaluates whether the structure and the dynamics of the committee can be improved? Is it time to review this again?

Chapter 3

The Investment Policy Statement

Like a good charter, the investment policy statement (IPS) sets clear expectations, defines roles and responsibilities, and establishes guiding principles while allowing sufficient flexibility for implementation to enable it to be the long-term guiding document it is intended to be.

An important step in establishing proper endowment-management procedures is to write a sound investment policy. An effective policy document will guide the efforts of trustees, investment committee members, staff, consultants, and OCIOs.

Why a Written Policy Is Critical

A formal investment policy is necessary, first and foremost, because fiduciary responsibility demands it. As noted in chapter 1, most fiduciaries are now legally held to a "prudent investor" standard. Experts agree that a prudent investor must have a well-reasoned, written investment policy that culminates in formal asset allocation guidelines.

Second, investment policy guidelines protect the endowment from market-driven departures from a sound long-term asset allocation policy. History teaches us that most market-driven responses are typically made at the wrong time and in exactly the wrong direction.

Third, an investment policy serves to inform *all* parties involved in an institution's endowment-management process, including the board of trustees, members of the investment committee, staff, consultants, and money managers. Providing new board and committee members with a copy of the investment policy aids their understanding of the objectives and guiding principles underpinning the endowment.

Characteristics of an Effective Policy

First, the best policies are specific enough that experienced outsiders could step in and implement them. There is a direct correlation between the clarity and precision of an investment policy and its usefulness. Measuring the implementation of policy guidelines and the attainment of policy objectives is also important. Broad, general pronouncements such as, "We seek to maximize returns without incurring undue risk," are of little value. It is more valuable to specify quantitative return objectives as well as risk parameters, set out the rationale for these objectives and parameters, and establish a clear benchmark against which performance is measured. The measurement of success should acknowledge the inevitability of short-term setbacks and adopt a reasonably long horizon for measuring performance, spanning a full market cycle.

Second, a strong investment policy includes sound justification for its objectives and guidelines. Explaining the basis for the policies adopted will help preempt questions from new committee members and stakeholders, and demonstrate explicitly that these policies are grounded in a robust analytical framework.

Third, the individual components of a good investment policy, which are discussed throughout the rest of this chapter, must be logically consistent and reinforce one another. This sounds obvious, yet we have seen many policies that include contradictory points.

Finally, an investment policy is meant to be long term in nature. It should not be changed frequently or in response to cyclical market shifts. A well-conceived policy should serve as a framework for at least three to five years.

Here are some items we recommend be included in an IPS (compiled through a number of sources, as well as our own experience):

Governance:
- Roles and responsibilities for various parties involved (committee, staff, outside firms)
- Date of last review and how frequently the policy will be reviewed
- A description of the asset pools/portfolios the policy covers

Statement of Investment Beliefs

Investment, Return, and Risk Objectives:
- Objectives for the portfolio—with prioritization on what is most important
- Constraints to be considered
- Identification of mission-aligned investment strategy (if there is one) and any DEI and/or ESG principles to be incorporated
- Other context to help frame the risk tolerance of the organization
- Target asset allocation (allowable asset classes with allowable ranges for each)
- Asset class rationales (and why they are included)
- Specific benchmarks for the portfolio and how performance will be measured

Risk Management:
- Risk measurement considerations
- Risk-management process
- Rebalancing procedures (timing and process)
- Specific appropriate metrics for risk management
- Liquidity requirements

Appendices:
- Spending policy

Statement of Investment Beliefs

It is increasingly common for groups to work to find common ground on key investment principles they believe in. This statement can help a group gain clarity on the use of active and/or passive portfolios, the level of investment in alternative investments, as well as other issues on which views can differ widely.

In our experience, it is also important to be explicit about which assets are covered by the policy, as well as the purpose of each pool of assets (if multiple pools are included). In addition, some institutions choose to include the spending policy as an appendix to the IPS and not in the body because any time the spending policy changes, the overall policy must be updated. Moreover, the spending policy is generally under the purview of another committee.

More information on investment policy statements can be found in the works included in the reading list in Appendix B. Two in particular should be consulted each time the policy statement is formally reviewed: Charles Ellis' *Investment Policy—How to Win the Loser's Game* and the CFA Institute's "Elements of an Investment Policy Statement for Institutional Investors."

Roles and Responsibilities

As we discussed extensively in the last chapter, success requires clarity on the roles and responsibilities of all of the parties involved in your investment program. One of the most important sections of the IPS is the roles and responsibilities.

Investment, Return, and Risk Objectives

Defining the appropriate objectives is a critical element of any investment program and thus an essential part of an investment policy statement. As noted earlier, objectives for investment returns must be specific and measurable so that the investment committee and the board can evaluate whether the portfolio is achieving the investment goals. These goals translate directly into a return objective and a policy benchmark and it is important to distinguish carefully between the two.

The overall-return objective of the endowment is to earn a total return (net of all investment-management fees and expenses) equal to or exceeding the spending rate plus the inflation rate. The level of return is quantified with reference to reasonable expectations for what financial markets are likely to yield; an assessment of the appropriate risk level to bear in order to generate returns; current and future budgetary requirements; and the strategic direction of the institution.

To achieve this return objective, the IPS should set out a strategic asset allocation for the endowment embodied in a *policy benchmark*, which is traditionally the weighted average of each of the benchmarks for each component of the portfolio, weighted as set forth in the long-term target allocation. This policy benchmark defines a portfolio structure expected to achieve the endowment's return objective within an acceptable amount of risk. The management of the endowment portfolio should aim to attain a total return matching or exceeding the portfolio's policy benchmark.

As part of ongoing monitoring, the IPS should encompass periodic reviews that address three questions:

1. Is the endowment's return objective still appropriate in light of the changing financial circumstances of the institution, and is it still a reasonable level of return to be expected from financial markets over the long run?

2. Did the strategic asset allocation embodied in the policy benchmark generate the return objective?

3. Did the investment process and implementation of the portfolio add or subtract value from the policy benchmark?

The objectives in the IPS should reflect the particular needs, characteristics, and resources of the institution. Every college or university must have a realistic understanding of its own financial situation and, accordingly, prioritize objectives among absolute returns, relative returns, and matching peer results. Having done so, it is important to adhere to this prioritization. We have observed that a committee that changes its priorities frequently is prone to return chasing, which is destructive to long-term value creation.

Risk Management: Striking the Right Balance

Risk management is ultimately a question of balance. To achieve a desired financial return, a variety of different types of risk must be assessed, taken, and controlled. The goal is to generate a return greater than a specific spending policy while keeping each type of risk within tolerable bounds. Risk is unavoidable: There is no compensation (in excess of a cash return) for holding a "risk-less" portfolio. Such a portfolio would fail to meet the endowment's long-term return objectives.

Investors face a wide range of risks that must be weighed using quantitative and qualitative assessments. Investing to meet a return objective necessarily involves price fluctuations (market risk), possible weaknesses in the investment decision-making process (behavioral risk), potential difficulties in the sale of investments (liquidity risk), trading with others who might not fulfill their obligations (counterparty risk), losses arising from errors or fraud (operational risk), the possibility that some investments will generate adverse publicity for the investor (reputational risk), and the possibility of misaligned incentives, either within the investor's institution or between the investor and third parties (conflicts-of-interest risk). There is also a real "opportunity cost" risk of being too cautious and investing so conservatively that the institution's endowment remains significantly smaller than would otherwise be the case. In drafting the IPS, the members of the investment committee should consider each of these risks, assess their tolerance for bearing them, and develop policies and procedures for their management.

Among the risks cited in the preceding paragraph, the most common focus of risk management is market risk, which is also the risk that is most amenable to quantitative measurement. Investment advisors use a set of statistical tools to quantify and manage risk in investment portfolios. These tools include standard statistical measures such as mean, variance, covariance, standard deviation, and correlation. The tools also include more specialized financial measures such as the Sharpe ratio, alpha, tracking error, and information ratio. Each of these concepts is described in the glossary of financial terms in Appendix C. Investment committee members should be encouraged to develop a working knowledge of the common measures of risk used in portfolio management.

Carefully assessing the acceptable level and types of risk taken in the endowment portfolio is a key responsibility of the committee. In designing the IPS, it is important to subject the long-term asset allocation to a battery of rigorous risk analytics to assess the range of investment outcomes that can be expected. These tests should assess whether the finances of the institution are resilient enough to weather a significant market downturn. The analysis of risk should also assess the impact of different operational scenarios and fluctuations on the need to tap endowment resources for unexpected budgetary needs. For some institutions, the impact on the institution from bad operational outcomes—like a significant enrollment shortfall—is potentially far more significant than volatility in the market value of the endowment. Such analysis warns committee members and other stakeholders of the potential for adverse outcomes, and thus should arm them against the temptation of panicked selling after a market crisis. These factors are laid out quite nicely in Walter Cabot's "The All-Important Relationship between the Board and Its Investment Committee," which we included in Appendix B as recommended reading.

Asset Allocation

Determining what percentage of the portfolio will be invested in various asset classes—stocks, bonds, real assets, private capital, hedge funds—is a core element of the IPS.

The policy document should set targets and allowable variation from the target for each asset class to permit a certain tolerance for market drift and to provide latitude for tactical asset allocation shifts as a means of adding value. In calibrating the size of these ranges, two considerations must be balanced. The ranges should be narrow enough to avoid the possibility that the risk and return characteristics of the actual portfolio sharply diverge from the committee's intentions when setting the long-term asset allocation policy, but they should be sufficiently wide to take into account market movements and allow meaningful asset allocation changes to take advantage of significant valuation anomalies across assets. Often, the implementation of a "new" model or new consultant, CIO, or OCIO begins with narrower ranges that widen as everyone grows more comfortable with the thought processes and capabilities.

An illustrative asset allocation and ranges for an endowment are provided in table 3.1, which shows that, even though U.S. or international equities may be targeted at a maximum of 30 percent, the overall equity ceiling limits the risk by having an upper band of 50 percent for equities.

Table 3.1 Illustrative Asset Allocation Target and Ranges

Category	Target	Allowable Range
Total Equity	40%	30–50%
U.S. Equities	20%	10–30%
International Equities	20%	10–30%
Total Alternatives	40%	30–50%
Hedged Strategies	20%	10–30%
Private Equity	20%	10–30%
Real Assets	5%	0–10%
TIPS	0%	0–5%
Commodities	0%	0–5%
Real Estate	5%	0–10%
Fixed Income	15%	10–30%
Investment Grade Debt	10%	5–20%
Other Debt	5%	0–10%
Cash	0%	0–10%
Other/Opportunistic	0%	0–10%

Note: Numbers do not reflect an actual client recommendation, but have been produced by the authors for purposes of example only.

Portfolio Building Blocks

One important item to be addressed as the committee designs the IPS should be ensuring that the total portfolio's risk and return characteristics achieve the long-term objectives for the portfolio. The total portfolio has a number of asset-class building blocks, each with its own characteristics and role in the total portfolio. The committee should arrive at a common understanding of the objective for each of these building blocks in the total portfolio. We provide the chief characteristics of the major asset classes here. Within each of these broad categories there are, of course, any number of finer distinctions.

Public equities are a key return engine, but also quite volatile. Risk in the equity market will dominate the portfolio unless offset by diversification with other assets.

Fixed income dampens volatility and provides liquidity. It can be diversified across the maturity and credit spectrum, as well as across U.S. and non-U.S. developed and emerging markets.

Hedge funds are a source of diversification and value added. Some treat hedge funds as levered strategies in the equity or credit markets and expect high risk and high, equity-like return. Others see hedge funds as a source of diversified value added and expect risk and return to fall between bonds and equities, but with little correlation to the rest of the portfolio. Be clear on what type of hedge fund portfolio the investment committee intends to target.

Real assets protect against unexpected inflation and help diversify the total portfolio risk and returns.

Private capital (venture capital and buyouts) have a high expected return, but are illiquid. Private capital investments are volatile, but not priced on a daily basis, or "marked to market" as frequently as publicly traded equities, helping to smooth out reported returns.

Opportunistic investments are investments that do not fit neatly into any of the other categories above, yet they are investments that may provide attractive return characteristics. Because the investment markets are dynamic, we believe there is value to creating a structure in your IPS that allows for some flexibility for investments to be made that may not have been anticipated at the time of the document's creation.

Student Investment Funds and University Venture Investments

Some institutions have created a separate endowed "Student Investment Fund" to be managed by business students as part of experiential learning curricula. Ideally, student-managed funds are donated expressly for student investment and designated for some purpose where continuity of funding may not be critical. Having a donor-designated fund for student investment provides assurance to other endowment donors that management of their gifts is not compromised. The investment committee, with support from faculty advisors, may provide guidance and feedback to students, but the pool is not managed as part of the regular portfolio.

Some research institutions designate a small portion of their endowment to invest in startups led by faculty, students, alumni, or staff to support commercialization of university research intellectual property, foster entrepreneurship, and yield a return on a par with their other private capital investments. The appeal of this for entrepreneurial board members and donors is clear, but the strategy entails significant risks. Boards may be favorably biased in their assessment of faculty or alumni startups, the exciting work of direct venture investing can distract from other critical board work, and the likelihood of outperforming venture funds is highly uncertain. Enthusiastic board members may also be interested in making side-by-side investments, a potential conflict of interest that can further increase risk. Boards that want to support university-related ventures may choose instead to raise funds designated specifically for investment in university ventures.

Rebalancing

Rebalancing is the process of adjusting or returning a portfolio toward the targets for asset allocation and level of market risk. Rebalancing is important because it keeps the institution's asset allocation from straying too far from policy guidelines. The IPS should therefore establish guidelines for portfolio rebalancing as a risk-management tool.

We recommend that the IPS specify that the portfolio's actual asset allocation be monitored regularly and rebalanced on a quarterly basis if the actual portfolio allocation diverges significantly from the current policy target. Interim rebalancing should be considered in the event of major market moves. The underlying exposures within each asset class should also be monitored regularly and, as in the case of asset-class rebalancing, be kept within reasonable bounds of the target allocation.

Rebalancing cannot always be accomplished fully and immediately. Illiquid asset classes such as venture capital, private equity, real estate, energy, and timber simply cannot be rebalanced in a short period of time. In these cases, it makes sense to offset any overweighting with a corresponding underweighting (and vice versa) in a related liquid strategy or asset class. For example, within real assets, allocations to relatively illiquid timber and energy investments can be adjusted by changing the allocation to more liquid Treasury Inflation-Protected Securities (TIPS), which are often included in the same asset class and have similar characteristics.

Portfolio and Asset-Class Benchmarks

Many investment committees confuse objectives and benchmarks. The IPS should distinguish clearly between them. In particular, it is important to remember that a benchmark is an aid for measuring the performance of a portfolio in the short term as well as the long term. The policy benchmark for the total portfolio is usually a weighted average of asset-class benchmarks, using the weights specified in the endowment's long-term target asset allocation. This should not be confused with a specific return objective, like achieving a 5 percent real return, which is necessarily long-term.

Benchmarks provide the standards against which investment performance is measured. An ideal benchmark is 1) clearly defined in advance; 2) representative of the targeted strategies, opportunities, or activities; 3) investable; 4) measurable; and 5) difficult but not impossible to beat. Good benchmarks meeting these criteria are available for virtually all traditional asset classes. Unfortunately, this is almost uniformly not the case for alternative asset classes. There are no investable benchmarks for hedge funds and private equity, yet we recognize that some comparator must be used in these categories. Hedge Fund Research (HFR) has developed some acceptable benchmarks for hedge funds; Burgiss and Thomson Reuters Cambridge Associates have done the same for private markets.

Investment committee members can compare actual returns with benchmarks to discover whether various investments are achieving their goals for relative performance. These performance comparisons often drive major decisions. Poor benchmarking leads to misleading performance analysis, which lowers the quality of subsequent decision making. Therefore, selection and use of the proper benchmark—whether for the entire endowment, an asset class, or a specific manager—are important and no changes should be made to the benchmarking methodology without the approval of the committee.

Measuring Success

The IPS should establish criteria for success and the appropriate frequency for reviews. Just as we recommend being clear about the difference between portfolio objectives (long-term goals reflecting the role of the endowment in the institution) and benchmarks (short- and long-term standards for assessing portfolio management) in the IPS, we recommend measuring the success of the two concepts individually. First, did the long-term strategic investment policy deliver performance that met objectives? Second, did the team accountable for overseeing the portfolio outperform the long-term policy benchmark?

Whether the endowment's investment policy benchmark has achieved its return objective should be assessed over rolling three- and five-year periods. Because market cycles tend to be long and performance can be exceptionally end-point dependent, this analysis necessarily requires an extended horizon. The policy benchmark represents the return that would have been earned if the endowment's actual asset allocation had matched the policy allocation and each asset class had earned the return of its assigned index.

The difference between the endowment's total return and its policy benchmark is the value added (or lost) through policy implementation. This comparison shows whether active management decisions, such as tactical asset allocation and security selection by active managers, have contributed to outperforming the policy target. Bear in mind, research and actual experience show that asset allocation and the variability of returns are the primary determinants of portfolio performance over the long term. In addition to comparing actual portfolio returns with the benchmark, it is important to compare volatility of the endowment's returns against the volatility of the returns of the policy benchmark.

A further measure of the success of the portfolio management is an analysis of whether the costs of the investment program have been both reasonable compared with industry standards and commensurate with performance. We have frequently observed that committees either do not pay enough attention to costs—allowing fees to absorb too high a share of the value added from managers—or pay too much attention to costs—avoiding managers with potentially superior net alpha (the value added relative to the benchmark) because their fees are deemed too high. High fees should only be paid for strategies that have a commensurately high level of likely value added relative to the benchmark. The ultimate measure of the success of the portfolio management is risk-adjusted, net-of-fee returns relative to the policy benchmark.

Responsible Investing

There has been rapid growth in the area of responsible investing as institutions seek to have their investment portfolio reflect their mission and values. Responsible investing takes many forms (see box below). The goals and scope of the various forms of responsible investing vary widely. Given the complexity of successfully designing and implementing a responsible investing program, we have devoted chapter 4 to discussing the process of determining the approach to responsible investing that best fits the needs and advances the mission and vision of your institution.

Multiple Approaches to Responsible Investing (RI)

Under the broad heading of "responsible investing" there are, at present, four primary approaches:

Socially responsible investing (SRI): A portfolio construction process that attempts to avoid investment in certain issuers or industries through negative screening according to defined guidelines and attempts to proactively invest in companies promoting desired social outcomes through positive screening.

Environmental, social, and governance (ESG): An investment practice that involves integrating the three ESG factors into fundamental investment analysis.

Divestment of fossil fuel: One movement that has gained a considerable amount of traction is fossil fuel divestment (FFD), which is a type of exclusionary screening strategy through which investors actively exclude companies involved with fossil fuels from their investment portfolio.

Impact investing: Investment in projects, companies, funds, or organizations with the express goal of generating and measuring positive economic, social, or environmental change alongside financial return.

There is not yet a completely standardized vocabulary of RI practices, as the field continues to evolve. At this point, SRI and ESG are the two most widely adopted approaches.

Here are a few things to consider:

- Each organization will define what it means by a "responsible" or "sustainable" investing strategy. Different institutions will define the terms "environmental," "socially responsible," or "optimal governance" differently. The development of these definitions and objectives, and their documentation, is critical to success.
- If an institution decides to pursue such a strategy, it will need to define an acceptable level of exposure to undesired companies. A zero-tolerance policy can be impractical to implement without significant opportunity costs, because it would prevent investment in broad indices on a passive basis, as well as alternative funds and other actively managed commingled vehicles that may be sources of high expected value added.
- It is important to understand whether an investment decision related to social goals affects the underlying risk and return characteristics of the portfolio by eliminating certain sectors or by significantly altering the portfolio's underlying risk factors. An analysis of the portfolio's underlying exposures can identify any unintended changes in its risk characteristics arising from the implementation of socially motivated investment decisions. Once identified, these unintended shifts in underlying risk can either be factored into the expectations for the portfolio's range of returns or offset.

Because of the items above and the need to follow good governance should you wish to align your portfolio to your mission, we devote the next chapter to the considerations involved in these approaches.

Summary

The first task of successful endowment management is to write a strong, appropriate, and effective investment policy statement. There are three minimal conditions to test whether an existing investment policy qualifies:

1. The policy meets fiduciary standards by addressing all of the important issues a prudent expert would address.

2. The policy objectives are realistic and aligned with the needs of the institution and the portfolio strategy outlined should allow the institution to achieve those objectives.

3. The written guidelines are specific and clear enough to guide those charged with implementing them and are easily understood by new committee members.

If you can confirm that yes, each of these assertions is true, the existing policy is probably strong. If not, now is the time to create an effective investment policy in fulfillment of the committee's and board's fiduciary responsibilities.

Key Questions for Boards

1. Does the institution's investment policy statement reflect the current best practices? If not, what steps can be taken toward doing so? If they vary from best practice, are these adjustments warranted?

2. Are board members in agreement with the priorities set for the portfolio's objectives as outlined in the investment policy statement? What can be done to improve communication with all relevant constituents concerning the priorities and objectives?

3. What has the investment committee done to maintain its focus on creating— and adhering to—an effective asset allocation policy?

4. Is there a clear distinction between return objectives and benchmarks in the IPS?

5. How often does the investment committee assess whether the asset allocation policy is appropriate given the endowment's requirements for returns and its risk profile?

6. What has the investment committee done to rigorously assess the portfolio's various risks? What has been done to make sure the committee is fully aware of the possible severity of bad outcomes?

Chapter 4

Aligning Your Portfolio with Your Mission

Valentina Glaviano

With the growing interest in mission-aligned investing and the increased emphasis on promoting diversity and inclusion in the investment management industry, boards are weighing the benefits of incorporating mission considerations in their investment process. AGB's maxim that the best boards and committees get the right people, focus on the right things, and do so in a respectful way is especially pertinent when considering whether and how to implement mission-aligned investing initiatives.

Step 1: Defining the Objectives

Although institutions typically have a clearly defined mission, converting that into actionable values requires collaboration with various constituents and represents the essential first step. The scope of factors comprising mission-aligned investing is quite broad and the mission-related objectives and preferences of different institutions are divergent. Most institutions that adopt mission-aligned investing are motivated by some combination of the following objectives: better aligning portfolios with stakeholders' values and norms; making a positive social or environmental impact; promoting diversity, equity and inclusion; reducing reputational risk; and generating higher returns. Which of these motivations to emphasize and the weight attached to each will vary across institutions and stakeholders. Defining what constitutes mission-aligned investing for your institution will therefore likely require careful consideration and potential compromise among the views of stewards and stakeholders. An open and transparent process is essential to achieve a broad consensus.

Given its importance, the decision to undertake mission-aligned investing requires careful evaluation by both the board and the investment committee. In this process, it is often helpful for the board, which holds the ultimate decision-making responsibility, to establish a **values alignment committee** (VAC) made up of two or three trustees as well as representatives from leadership, faculty, students, and donors to conduct a detailed review of the values alignment initiatives that should be considered. Because values alignment is likely to be an ongoing journey for the institution, it may be advisable to make this committee permanent. The VAC should be part of the board of trustees and not simply a subset of the investment committee, because it should reflect the views of the institution. In most colleges or universities, the mission and values are clear. If not, the VAC should be charged with conducting stakeholder interviews to seek the views of all constituents on such questions as:

- What values do we believe align with the mission of the institution?
- What role will diversity and inclusion have in these efforts? (See "Governance Considerations for Diversity and Inclusion Investment Initiatives.")
- How can the institution align its operations and investments with these values? Should this alignment be limited to investments, or be integral to all aspects of the institution's operations? (See "The Importance of Alignment.")
- What concrete changes should we seek? And, what is the outcome we are seeking through those changes?

Governance Considerations for Diversity and Inclusion Investment Initiatives

Diversity and inclusion are often implicit in mission-aligned investment initiatives and can be integrated in the RI program. Efforts to promote diversity and inclusion raise additional governance considerations that are distinct from other responsible investing goals.

Identifying Diverse and Inclusive Investment Managers
Importantly, we believe that many share a common goal that the investment management industry reflect the level of diversity in the world in which we live. As David Swensen, in one of his last letters as the CIO of the Yale endowment wrote: "Success will be measured by hiring, training, mentoring, and retaining women and minorities for positions on the investment teams. . . ."

As in the case of RI, there is no agreed-upon standard of what constitutes adequate levels of diversity and inclusion. The investment committee will need to consider how to define and measure the desired level of diversity across managers and how they will choose to engage with managers to seek progress. Diversity initiatives, both within the investment management industry and across institutional investors, are evolving quickly. To put your institution in the best place and reflect the daily learnings of other thoughtful institutions, we would suggest you educate yourself on the recent developments of your peers.

Armed with these definitions, a first step would then be to take stock of the level of diversity represented in your existing managers and service providers and send a questionnaire to them to collect information on them. There are many good resources upon which institutions can build the diversity questionnaires such as the CFA Institute's Diversity Data Collection Template.

As in the case of other RI initiatives, there will inevitably be some compromises and need for flexibility in implementing the diversity and inclusion program. Diversity in the investment management industry is currently limited and is unevenly spread across asset classes. Diverse managers frequently have fewer assets under management and shorter track records than others. Some institutions may choose to limit the amount, in dollars or as a percentage, that they can represent of a manager's business, and this may then lead to a large number of additional managers to oversee as institutions seek to improve allocations to diverse managers.

Institutions may choose different approaches to improve diversity. Some may choose to set targets and others may choose to seek progress from where they are today. In any case, encouraging existing managers to increase their emphasis on diversity will be an important part of any diversity initiative.

David Swensen emphasized the importance of opening up possibilities to those not traditionally well represented in the investment industry. "By and large, the number of experienced investment professionals is fixed. We do not solve the larger problem of underrepresentation by recruiting diverse candidates from other investment organizations. Such position shuffling is a zero-sum game, doing nothing to improve diversity of the overall industry. Yet, if we hire and train diverse individuals early in their careers, we can expand the numbers of talented, diverse investment management professionals."

Promoting Diversity More Broadly
In addition to promoting diversity in the investment management industry, many institutions also seek to encourage diversity more broadly across all corporations and institutions.

To this end, many institutions seek to understand how their managers are measuring and monitoring the diversity of leadership of the companies in which they invest. Some ask their managers to provide annual reports on the degree of diversity represented in their portfolio.

Further, many institutions are looking to promote diversity through dedicated investments with managers who invest with organizations led by diverse entrepreneurs. Here too, some compromises and flexibility may be needed.
- Many of these diverse entrepreneurs will not have the same access to networks and thus operational, management, and legal resources that one typically sees in other start-ups.
- Many of these entrepreneurs, while often seeking a double bottom line, are also seeking to promote a greater good in their community that would categorize investments with them as impact and thus would necessitate that the institution define an impact investing initiative.

Given these challenges, it is important to seek diversity progress through an open and transparent process that weighs how best to promote diversity while also ensuring that the portfolio achieves its investment objectives and maintains appropriate due diligence standards. The governance principles that we describe in this chapter for RI programs apply equally to diversity and inclusion initiatives.

The goal of the VAC should be to define the objectives of mission alignment. Once defined, the investment committee would be charged with determining the optimal approach to reflect these objectives in the investment portfolio. With the recognition that mission-aligned investing will be an evolving process, many investment committees have found it helpful to form a subcommittee, the responsible investment subcommittee (RIC) made up of investment committee members who have RI expertise or are committed to gaining that expertise.

The main benefit of the VAC's work derives from its canvassing the views of a broad spectrum of stakeholders. This process of broad consultation serves a critical information-gathering function. An open and transparent process will promote support for the mission while also serving an educational purpose, informing key constituents about the values of the institution, and suggesting ways that these values are being reflected in the institution's operations and investments. It may also be helpful at this stage to engage a legal expert in fiduciary duty to review key responsibilities outlined in all of the institution's governance documents as well as your state's UPMIFA with the VAC and the investment committee. UPMIFA allows for mission considerations when assessing fiduciary duty and carves out investment assets that have a primary program or mission purpose, as opposed to an investment purpose from the traditional investment-prudence analysis. In addition, as an element of its prudence analysis, UPMIFA invokes the consideration of "an asset's special relationship or special value, if any, to the charitable purposes of the institution."

Step 2: Reflecting the Mission in the Investment Portfolio

Once broadly defined, the next step of the process is to determine how best to align the investment portfolio with the mission. At this stage, the values and broad mission objectives are analyzed, taking into account practical constraints. This stage of the process seeks answers to the following key questions:

- What is the best way to reflect the mission and values in the investment portfolio?
- What impact do we think this will have on our current portfolio? Are we comfortable with that?
- Should the alignment of the investment portfolio with the mission be phased? If so, over what period? (See "The Ongoing Journey")
- Is it acceptable to incur additional fees and expenses to achieve mission alignment? If so, what is a reasonable threshold of additional expense?
- Is it acceptable to forgo potential returns to align the investment portfolio with the institution's mission and values? If so, what is the order of magnitude of any opportunity cost?

There are a variety of approaches to aligning the portfolio with the mission, each with its relative merits. It is important to weigh the pros and cons of each approach and, to the extent possible, its potential impact on portfolio returns and costs.

Key Questions for Investment Committee and Representatives of the VAC:

Possible Paths to Alignment
- What is the best way to achieve each of the mission-alignment goals? Should this objective be implemented using divestment, negative/positive screening, active ownership, or some combination of these techniques? (See table 4.1 featuring a mission-aligned goals sample matrix.)

  The actions in the table that follows can be defined as:

  - Divestment is sometimes referred to as negative screening. It refers to defining securities that the institution will sell from their current portfolio and screen out going forward based on their overall business activity, defined percentage of revenue or philosophy. For example, an institution might want to divest from fossil fuel companies that do not have a certain percentage of their revenue from renewable energy sources or one that denies climate change is a problem.
  - Positive screening is the process of finding companies that score highly on environmental, social, and governance (ESG) factors that align with the institution's values relative to their peers. For example, a screen might be used to target only companies, meeting a manager's investment criteria, that also meet specified diversity criteria across their organization.

Table 4.1 Mission-Aligned Goals Sample Matrix

Value	Divestments	Positive Screening	Active Ownerships	Impact
Climate Change	✓	✓	✓	✓
Diversity	✓	✓	✓	✓
Human Rights	✓		✓	

- Active ownership involves investors working with portfolio companies to improve how they manage or disclose "ESG" factors across their business. It can be a proactive strategy by institutional shareholders, most often in collaboration with other like-minded institutions, to encourage a business to modify their practices in line with the desired values those institutional shareholders want to promote. For example, concerns over climate change have led some investors through collaborative efforts with networks such as CERES to engage the management of securities issuers on strategies to reduce their emissions and in some cases introduce shareholder resolutions.
- Impact, while similar to positive screening in that it refers to seeking to invest in companies that positively align with an institution's values, goes deeper in that it refers to companies that exist specifically to promote an issue or solve a problem, sometimes, but not necessarily, at the expense of traditional returns. For example, impact investments can be made in venture capital funds that seek to solve the funding challenges that often face diverse entrepreneurs.
- Have past divestment or active investment campaigns been successful? What made them successful?
- What is the scope of the change being sought by aligning investments with the mission? What is the time frame for achieving the desired change? What complementary measures might be needed to achieve this aim? (See "Divestment Considerations.")
- How have other institutions with similarly sized investment pools and similar objectives structured their program of mission alignment? What are the lessons of their experience? (See "Many Paths to Values-Aligned Investing.")
- Does taking action align with the board's fiduciary responsibility of ensuring that the institution sustains its mission for the long term and represents the views of all constituents, including donors?
- Are there any donor agreements in place that would prohibit steps to align the portfolio with the mission? If so, how do you need to adjust your approach? Might you need to create a new portfolio that invests differently and for which you fundraise specifically?
- How will planned actions in the investment portfolio affect your operations? (See "Divestment Considerations.")

Divestment Considerations

Several case studies and academic research reports demonstrate how divestment can sometimes have unforeseen and even counterproductive consequences. In weighing divestment as a mechanism for implementing mission-aligned investing, it is important to bear these real-life considerations in mind.

Efficacy

In the 1980s, divestment from South Africa by U.S. endowments and other institutional investors globally helped affect the desired change of eliminating apartheid by raising awareness of atrocities in South Africa. The fact that divestment spurred continued protests against apartheid led corporations and governments to boycott and impose sanctions against South Africa, putting pressure on the apartheid regime. The economic pressure that was the direct result of the boycotts and sanctions is credited with toppling the apartheid regime not the divestment campaigns themselves.

Many recent studies have suggested that divestment from fossil fuels by endowments and foundations might not have the same effect because they are not the marginal investor and may have a negligible impact on the share price. A policy of fossil fuel divestment would benefit from complementary steps to reduce demand for fossil fuels while supporting conservation efforts and regulatory initiatives to curb the use of fossil fuels. Complementary measures include mobilizing public support for increased regulation or boycotts of fossil fuel companies, pressure to end governmental subsides and support to fossil fuel producers, carbon taxes, as well as subsidies to encourage consumers to switch to clean and renewable energy sources. (PERI, University of Massachusetts, Amherst: Economics and Climate Justice Activism: Assessing the Fossil Fuel Divestment Movement.)

Unforeseen Consequences

With respect to the economic consequences of divestment, a 2019 Harvard study titled *Examining the Impact of Fossil Fuel Divestment on University Endowments* found that "The economic result of . . . . early divestment campaigns (in tobacco companies) often had a negligible impact on the companies within the targeted sector. While the share values in divested companies dropped significantly in a few cases, most did not. In fact, shares in these companies were merely reallocated to share purchasers who were not concerned with the social movement prompting divestment from these companies. While divestment movements can be successful, this success rarely results in permanently reducing any firm's share value, because other investors, who are unconcerned by the social considerations of the divestment campaign, can buy the divested shares, perhaps at a reduced rate. For example, 'sinvestors'—who invest exclusively in sectors like alcohol, tobacco, firearms, and gambling—can wait in the offing for a divestment campaign to target a firm and scoop up the divested shares at a reduction in share value to hold the assets until they become more profitable again. If the divesting party sells low and the sinvestor buys the divested stock low as well, the valuations of the divested stock will remain relatively stable and unaffected by this reallocation."

Donor Relations

A university endowment in the Northwest was pressured by students and faculty including some who had produced highly regarded work around climate change, to divest from fossil fuels. However, when the development team did an evaluation of the donors, they found that a significant portion of substantial donors were involved in the fossil fuel industry and did not look upon divestment favorably. Given that this institution was already under financial strain prior to the pandemic and could not afford to lose support in the midst of implementing a strategic plan, it was determined that divestment would risk the long-term viability of the institution, so they opted to leverage the connectivity of their donors to employ investor engagement initiatives.

Impacts on the Broader Institution

The 2019 Harvard study quoted above found that "In the last decade, many index funds have increased their holdings in fossil fuel companies' securities such that fossil fuel companies now make up a large part of major benchmark indices." Thus, one could argue that a fossil fuel divestment initiative by the endowment's investment portfolio should also require that index funds be removed from the institution's pension plans, and further, that investment in the debt issues of such companies should also be prohibited across the reserve and cash management accounts of the institution. Such steps would raise a number of questions. How would removing index funds from defined contribution plans affect the participants? Would alternatives entail higher direct and opportunity costs? If so, is there a limit to the incremental costs that the institution would be willing to bear to achieve mission alignment?

Assessing Implications on Portfolio Returns

- What are your return expectations? Do you expect higher returns, similar returns, or are you willing to give up some return in exchange for better mission alignment? If so, how much?
- Is there enough evidence to evaluate the potential consequences on returns?
- How will you measure success both at the portfolio level and in the case of each strategy? What is the appropriate time frame for this evaluation?
- How vulnerable is the institution to the potential for increased return volatility or lower returns? Does this vulnerability influence either the amount allocated to mission-aligned investing or the nature of the strategies adopted?

Many Paths to Mission-Aligned Investing

Every endowment faces unique circumstances and targets different objectives when pursuing mission-aligned investing. When drawing lessons from the experience of others, it is important to bear in mind these potentially divergent circumstances and objectives. For example, contrast the Fossil Fuel Divestment initiative implemented by Pitzer College with the direction Grinnell College took.

Grinnell is, first and foremost, committed to supporting those who would not otherwise have the opportunity to go to college. In order to do so, Grinnell funds a much higher percentage of its operating budget through the endowment. Any adverse effects that aligning the investment strategy with values might have could materially affect Grinnell's ability to attain its mission. Pitzer College, in contrast, is one of the "greenest" schools in the country and one of the first to have an environmental studies major. Being a leader on environmental issues is core to Pitzer's identity. Moreover, Pitzer's reliance on its endowment to fund the budget is relatively small. These factors give Pitzer greater latitude to risk the possibility of foregoing some return as a result of aligning the endowment portfolio with its core values and mission.

Mission alignment does not need to be viewed as an all-or-nothing initiative. For example, if the goal is divestment from fossil fuels, eliminating all fossil fuel investments from the endowment can be phased over time to avoid undue disruption to the portfolio. The phased divestment of fossil fuels could be complemented with investments in renewable energy companies.

When learning from the activities of others, it is important to study institutions that are similar in size, circumstances, and objectives. Access to different investment options varies significantly with size, with larger portfolios typically having more opportunities for customization than smaller asset pools. The uneven availability of investment options may limit opportunities to add value. For example, the Harvard study quoted earlier found that smaller institutions suffered a negative impact from fossil fuel divestment, while midsized to larger institutions experienced no impact and, in some cases, a positive impact on returns. These results are period specific and different time horizons may yield different conclusions.

There are a number of organizations that support institutional initiatives in responsible investing by providing a library of information, data, and suggested best practices. Some of the more prominent examples include the Intentional Endowments Network (IEN), the UN Principals for Responsible Investment (UNPRI), CERES, the Global Impact Investing Network, the Forum for Sustainable and Responsible Investment (USSIF), the Interfaith Center on Corporate Responsibility, and the Catholic Impact Investing Collaborative (CIIC).

Step 3: Prepare to Implement

The implementation phase could raise challenges that may necessitate a reassessment of the objectives and scope of the mission-aligned investing initiative. Recognition at the outset that some flexibility in implementation will likely be necessary should facilitate the process. The investment committee and its advisors are best placed to assess the tradeoffs and practical considerations raised by implementing a mission-aligned investment strategy. They should be given sufficient latitude to find the optimal balance between what is sought and what is possible.

Key Questions for Investment Committee members and representatives of the VAC

Governance Considerations

- Are there clear guidelines on how to measure progress in aligning the portfolio with the mission?
- Have underlying managers been given clear mission-related guidelines? Have we established a suitable benchmark against which to measure each manager's progress?
- Will a significant portion of the underlying managers need to be changed?
- Will the investment oversight and implementation model need to be changed to accommodate a comprehensive view of the portfolio exposures and characteristics at all times? Will this necessitate additional staffing, or changes away from an advisory to a discretionary model?

Return Considerations

- Are there benefits to aligning only part of the portfolio with the mission? A partial approach might facilitate implementation, provide scope for experimentation, leave open opportunities for donors who might not share mission goals, or reduce risks to the entire portfolio.
- If return expectations are higher or equal, do you expect those to be achieved by the investments directly or through factor overlay, portfolio completion, and risk mitigation strategies? Does the investment oversight structure in place allow for those strategies to be employed effectively?
- Is there a procedure for measuring the impact on management fees and returns arising from aligning the portfolio with the mission?
- Is there a framework for reporting the results of the mission alignment initiative to stakeholders?
- If the funds are governed by UPMIFA, how does sacrificing return align with the total-return rule to which fiduciaries of institutional funds must adhere, and which precludes consideration of factors that do not directly benefit the beneficiary? How will you define, quantify, measure, and track the direct benefit to the beneficiaries?

Divestment Considerations

- What are the criteria for divesting from firms? Are these criteria easy to apply? Is third-party assistance needed to define and apply the divestment criteria?
- How much latitude for judgment should be provided in applying the divestment criteria? How will unintended or undesirable outcomes be treated?

Active Ownership Considerations

- Are there adequate resources to have an effective shareholder engagement program? Is there scope for joining with like-minded institutions to increase the impact and share the costs of engagement?
- Should securities held for shareholder engagement be held in a segregated portfolio or within the endowment portfolio? How will the return of these shares be monitored and benchmarked?
- Should the endowment invest with activist strategies that are seeking to affect changes in key companies that align with those we would seek to effect? Can the endowment afford to give up the liquidity necessary to do so and, if so, what will be the short- and long-term implications on returns? What is the differential in the extra costs of such investment strategies versus the resources the institution would need to dedicate to mount an effective shareholder engagement program on its own?

  Note: Investors commonly assume that an ESG manager or a team managing an ESG strategy will align its proxy voting with the responsible investing mandate of the strategy, but that is not always the case, especially with highly customized strategies.

Step 4: Document

An institution's investment policy statement (IPS) should provide a framework for outlining in as much detail as possible what role mission and values play in the management of the portfolio. The IPS should define the broad objectives of the mission-aligned investing program, specify the entities responsible for implementing the initiative, establish expectations for monitoring and reporting on results, and set the timeline for periodic reviews of the mission-alignment program.

Core Responsible Investing Beliefs

The IPS should include a mission statement that lays out the values embodied in the Responsible Investing Program. It should also include background information on the process of consultation undertaken to define the values inherent in the mission and specify that a similar process should be followed in subsequent reviews of the program. A time frame for periodic review should also be indicated.

Governance

The process for overseeing the implementation of the RI initiatives should be formalized in the IPS, which should set out the following elements of the RI initiative's governance:

- Specify how the RI initiative is to be implemented, including negative or positive screens, shareholder engagement, or some combination.
- Establish guidelines for monitoring the implementation of the RI program.
- Define lines of responsibility and accountability for implementing the RI program.
- Specify how the RI program's objectives will be communicated to third-party investment managers and advisors.
- Describe success criteria and a process for monitoring and reporting.
- Establish expectations for the timing and scope for subsequent reviews of the RI objectives.

Investment Guidelines, Return and Risk Objectives

Setting the guidelines for implementing the RI initiatives into the investment portfolio is often a two-step process. The investment guidelines specific to the overall portfolio and each asset class in the portfolio should be established first, as those are the drivers to achieving the investment goals. This involves not only the allocation to public versus private equities but also the determination of what types of strategies (such as active or passive) and vehicles (such as SMAs or commingled funds) will be used in implementation.

The second step is to define how the RI initiative should be implemented, and specify whether the RI program applies to all or part of the portfolio.

- Set goals for the timing of completing the current RI implementation.
- Define acceptable ranges for mission alignment by asset class, including any exceptions.
- Describe any changes in benchmarks or any additional benchmarks that will be needed to assess performance, measure relative risk, and monitor the portfolio's alignment with the RI goals.
- Address how undesired changes to the portfolio's underlying exposures and risk characteristics that arise from the RI program will be monitored and mitigated.
- Provide guidance on the latitude for making RI investments that have lower expected returns than conventional investments.
- Define the period over which the investment success of the program will be judged.

  Note: Performance benchmarks have implications for risk and tracking error and therefore, should be both investable and applicable to reflect the RI initiatives being employed. However, because it is a best practice to evaluate the consequence of the decisions, we would suggest two comparisons: First, relative to an ESG benchmark that best represents each RI initiative; second, against a widely accepted benchmark that is typically used as the standard for the asset class. These comparisons allow the committee to measure the implications of your RI initiatives and disentangle the impact attributable to the performance of individual managers, and the impact of the RI initiative itself.

Step 5: Monitor

Once an RI program is established, the investment committee should monitor its implementation as part of its regular responsibilities for supervising portfolio management and performance. A formal evaluation of the RI program should be undertaken at least annually. This review should include a status report on the extent of the RI implementation throughout the portfolio; an estimate of the impact of the program on portfolio returns, risk, fees, and expenses; and an assessment of whether the RI program is furthering the mission objectives and values of the institution. Monitoring should be undertaken at the level of each manager, asset class, and the total portfolio.

Given the lack of widely accepted standards at present, we recognize that monitoring is likely to be a challenge. Corporate reporting on environmental, social, and governance (ESG) practices is inconsistent. There are calls for the SEC to establish ESG materiality and reporting standards, which may help clarify standards. Without widely accepted standards, firms ranking corporations' ESG performance apply inconsistent criteria and, as a consequence, assign corporations divergent and at times contradictory ESG scores. Investment managers in the same asset class might use different ESG benchmarks, further complicating monitoring and reporting.

Impact is even harder to measure and usually requires a third-party service. A major challenge is the lack of quantifiable metrics. Additionally, while many frameworks for measurement exist, there are currently no industry-wide standards for impact reporting and measurement.

To evaluate the results of the responsible investing program, consider the following questions:

- Are the short- and long-term effects of your RI initiatives generating the desired results? Are you able to document these results in reports to stakeholders?
- Are there unexpected positive or negative consequences resulting from your RI initiatives? How will you address these consequences?
- What are you learning from your efforts? How should these learnings shape your RI initiatives and policy going forward?
- What new learnings can you glean from similar institutions with similar RI initiatives and goals?

- Do any of these learnings change your core RI beliefs, or suggest changes to the means and timing of their implementation?
- Is the RI program remaining current with best practices and available strategies and techniques?
- Do the benefits of the RI program outweigh its costs? Is this tradeoff acceptable?

Step 6: Revisit

Given the rapidly changing environment around available investment solutions, it is prudent to develop a plan for revisiting the scope, objectives, and implementation of the mission alignment initiative. Periodic reviews are likely to identify improvements to the initiative building on experience in its implementation. Such reviews would also open the possibility to accommodate changing preferences and priorities.

Summary

As with any major initiative, the alignment of the endowment portfolio with the mission will likely encounter unforeseen consequences. A flexible approach to implementation that is able to adapt to both opportunities and challenges as they arise should be integral to the initiative's design. Recognizing from the outset that there may be tradeoffs and developing an approach for addressing them will go far in smoothing implementation and allowing for the adaptation to evolutions that are occurring. Clearly defined objectives and a way to monitor progress toward their achievement are also essential. Ultimately, an open process of consultation and transparent reporting on implementation will contribute to maintaining support for the endowment and confidence in those managing it.

Chapter 5

Portfolio Construction

As we have discussed in chapter 3, the investment policy statement is the strategic roadmap for managing the endowment and contains many strategies and policies developed by the trustees and staff after due deliberation. Determining the strategic asset allocation for all investment portfolios, most notably, the endowment, is a key responsibility of the investment committee. Over the long term, the asset mix will be the most significant determinant of whether the endowment achieves its expected returns. To be "right," the asset mix must be based on sound assumptions, have a high probability of achieving the endowment's targeted returns, and be structured efficiently, generating returns from the market without taking on undue risk.

Asset allocation determines the share of the portfolio that will be allocated to each asset class or strategy—public equities, bonds, real assets, private capital, and hedge funds. The asset allocation policy will be the main driver of returns. But just how significant is asset allocation? There has long been confusion over this matter.

Importance of Asset Allocation

The awareness of the general importance of asset allocation is due to Gary Brinson, Randolph Hood, and Gil Beebower's 1986 article, "Determinants of Portfolio Performance." They concluded that, on average, 93.6 percent of the variability in a portfolio's performance over time is the result of asset allocation policy. Although this study was conducted many years ago, it remains the most important study about the importance of asset allocation.

One persistent source of confusion in interpreting the article is the relative importance of strategic asset allocation (i.e., the long-term investment policy) versus tactical asset allocation (i.e., deviations from the long-term policy due to portfolio drift or explicit active tilts). Brinson et al. found that strategic asset allocation policy explains the 93.6 percent of a portfolio's variability over time. They found that the impact of tactical asset allocation explained only an incremental amount of portfolio-return variability and that these tactical shifts detracted, on average, 0.66 percent from performance. In other words, the average institution's attempts to time asset classes made little difference to the portfolio's overall pattern of returns and were actually somewhat counterproductive.

Roger Ibbotson and Paul Kaplan addressed these issues in their 2000 article, "Does Asset Allocation Policy Explain 40, 90, or 100 Percent of Performance?" They found that, on average, about 100 percent of the investment return is explained by asset allocation policy. According to Roger Ibbotson, "This is so because, on average, active management (market timing and manager selection) adds nothing. This does not say you should not use active management. We are talking about averages, and on average, active management adds nothing." It is thus essential that investment committees focus on the strategic issue of determining an appropriate asset allocation policy for the endowment.

Asset Allocation Trends

For some time, colleges and universities increasingly have been investing in alternative investments—especially hedge funds and private equity. As seen in successive editions of the *NACUBO–Commonfund Study of Endowments* and later the *NACUBO–TIAA Study of Endowments* over the years, the amounts allocated to alternatives (defined here to include investments in private capital, hedge funds, real estate, natural resources, distressed debt, and other forms of private investments) by the average nonprofit institution have grown steadily. The figures reported are dollar-weighted averages and are thus heavily influenced by the largest endowments (which have the greatest allocations to alternative investments) and only marginally affected by the smaller endowments, which have much lower allocations.

Indeed, there is a substantial difference in asset allocation to alternatives between large and small endowments, with the institutions with more than $1 billion in endowments having a greater than 50 percent allocation (on average) to alternatives and institutions with less than $100 million having approximately 25 percent. Moreover, the allocations of alternatives by smaller institutions look very different from those of larger institutions. Compared to their larger counterparts, smaller endowments have a much higher allocation to hedge funds within alternatives and a commensurately smaller allocation to private capital. The wide divergence in allocations across and within asset classes is one factor explaining the variations in returns among endowments of different sizes. The reasons for these divergent allocations to alternatives include varying liquidity requirements, risk tolerances, management capabilities and manager access across endowments of different sizes.

Guides for Portfolio Construction

Modern portfolio theory and practice. Designing an endowment's investment policy rests on constructing a portfolio with the desired risk and return characteristics. As we saw in the first chapter, an endowment's risk and return targets should be aligned with the spending policy, broader finances, and the strategic direction of the institution. As we have just discussed, the asset mix in endowment portfolios varies greatly across endowments of different sizes and has varied significantly over time. What determines the appropriate mix of assets within each portfolio? How can an investment committee know that the asset allocation in its endowment is the right one? Modern portfolio theory provides an analytical framework to address these questions.

Modern portfolio theory helps guide portfolio construction by focusing on three characteristics of each asset class or building block used to construct a portfolio: the asset's expected return, risk (variability of expected returns), and correlations to other assets (the degree to which asset returns move together). A key insight of modern portfolio theory is the power of diversification, often called the only "free lunch" in investments. By combining assets that are not highly correlated in a portfolio, we can reduce the variability of the portfolio's returns. Thus, the risk (often measured by standard deviation of returns) of a portfolio is not just a function of the risk of the assets considered in isolation. Portfolio risk also reflects the correlation across assets—the degree to which the returns of different assets move together. As long as the assets in a portfolio are not perfectly correlated, the observed risk of a portfolio is always lower than the weighted average risk of the assets that comprise it.

Following modern portfolio theory, we should aim to construct portfolios that represent an efficient tradeoff between risk and return in the sense that no other combination of assets will yield a higher return for a given level of risk or a lower risk for a given expected return. These portfolios are identified using an optimization technique.

Derivation of capital market assumptions. Since assumptions about the future risk, return, and correlation of various asset classes are the basis for constructing efficient portfolios, it is essential to develop a well-founded and realistic set of capital market assumptions. Most practitioners base their capital market assumptions on actual historical data to derive long-term expectations consistent with economic and financial-market equilibrium. The focus is identifying the mix of risk, return, and correlation characteristics that is consistent with market equilibrium. This is important because the planning horizon for endowment investing is very long. Given this long horizon, every effort is made to ensure that the capital market assumptions used are not too influenced by a particular point in a market cycle. These historical observations are often adjusted to account for secular trends and to compensate for data inadequacies, including those arising from irregular pricing in illiquid markets.

Some service providers estimate expected returns for each asset class using a global capital asset pricing model (CAPM) framework. (See table 5.1 for an example of the output of this methodology.) In CAPM, the expected return is the compensation earned from taking systematic, non-diversifiable risk. Because of their long-term horizon, asset-class assumptions typically change very little from year to year, but gradual changes do occur as secular trends unfold. For example, correlations across most asset classes have increased, primarily because of globalization and the integration of world capital markets, and this has been incorporated into many forward-looking estimates.

Table 5.1 Illustrative Long-Term Nominal Expected Return and Risk

Asset Class	Return	Volatility
Equities		
U.S. Equity	8.1%	16.8%
Developed Non-U.S. Equity	9.0%	17.1%
Emerging Markets Equity	10.0%	21.5%
Alternatives		
Private Equity	11.0%	23.6%
Directional Hedge Funds	7.0%	9.8%
Market Neutral Hedge Funds	3.9%	7.9%
Real Assets		
Real Estate	5.3%	10.8%
TIPS	4.0%	4.4%
Commodities	7.0%	24.6%
Fixed Income		
U.S. Investment Grade Fixed Income	4.0%	5.9%
High Yield	6.0%	11.2%
Non-U.S. Fixed Income	4.2%	5.3%
Cash	2.5%	0.0%

Note: Numbers do not reflect actual capital markets data but have been produced by the authors for purposes of example only.

One source of persistent confusion in interpreting these expected returns is that they are often expressed using two different calculation conventions: arithmetic average and geometric average.

The arithmetic average is the simple averaging calculation that we commonly use in everyday life. The geometric growth rate reflects the compounded growth of the portfolio and reflects the basis for calculating the value of the portfolio's assets. As seen in table 5.2, the geometric average is always less than the arithmetic average for risky assets, with the difference increasing for assets that are more volatile. Even with equal arithmetic average returns, the portfolio with the lower return volatility will leave you with a lower dollar value over time.

Table 5.2 Comparing Geometric Averages to Arithmetic Averages

	Starting Value	After Year 1	After Year 2	Arithmetic Average	Geometric Average
High Volatility Portfolio	$100	$150 (return +50%)	$75 (return -50%)	0%	-13.4%
Low Volatility Portfolio	$100	$110 (return +10%)	$99 (return -10%)	0%	-0.5%

Both conventions are correct when used appropriately in portfolio analytics, but the different conventions often lead to confusion when comparing estimates from different sources. The numbers in the expected return exhibit above are arithmetic averages.

In addition to specifying the expected equilibrium return and risk of each asset class, it is also essential to set a realistic estimate of the correlation of each asset with others in the portfolio. This quantifies the diversification benefit of combining portfolios in different ways. Like the risk and return characteristics just discussed, equilibrium correlation expectations are also informed by history and should avoid being overly influenced by particular points in the cycle. Many assets are quite closely correlated. U.S. and non-U.S. equity markets, for example, often move closely together. Others, like U.S. equities and U.S. Treasuries, are driven by different factors and are less closely correlated.

Some practitioners also adjust the long-term equilibrium-expected market returns (or beta) to incorporate active return added value (or alpha) assumptions. The assumed added value from active management should be based on the institution's historical experience, and they should be conservative. Applying these alpha assumptions to each asset class provides a more complete basis for constructing a range of optimal portfolios, as the expected returns for each asset class used in the optimization reflect both alpha (added value) and beta (market) sources of return. Each committee member should understand the methodology and if alpha is included or not included.

Efficient Frontier Analysis

Using capital market inputs, the next step is to construct an "efficient frontier" of diversified portfolios through an optimization process that identifies the mix of asset classes that maximizes expected return at each level of risk. (See figure 5.1.) The efficient frontier represents the expected risk and return of optimally allocated portfolios. A portfolio on the efficient frontier has the maximum expected return for its level of risk. Portfolios falling below the efficient frontier are suboptimal because it is possible to achieve a higher level of return for a given level of risk or the same expected return with lower risk.

Once optimal portfolios are identified along the efficient frontier, the final step in the process is to select an asset mix from the efficient frontier that is consistent with the endowment's investment objectives and constraints—that is, one expected to deliver the desired level of return at the lowest level of risk. This allocation is formalized into a strategic policy benchmark that guides the management of the portfolio and provides a standard to use in evaluating the portfolio's performance.

Figure 5.1 The Efficient Frontier

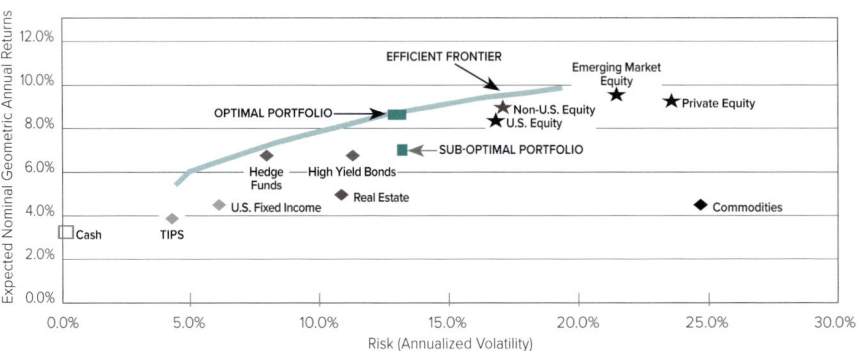

From figure 5.1, it is easy to see that some portfolios are "better" than others because they have a higher return for the same level of risk or the same return at a lower level of risk.

Sensitivity. The output of an efficient frontier analysis is very sensitive to the inputs. Small changes in input assumptions often produce big changes in the composition of portfolios that the model identifies as "efficient." Changes in the estimates of expected returns have far greater impact than do changes in the estimates of standard deviations, which in turn are more significant than errors in the estimates of correlations.

Since the inputs can only be estimated, and even small changes in these estimates can lead to large changes in the optimal weights, why use efficient frontier analysis? This is a legitimate question. Certainly, such analysis is only one tool and should never be the only means for determining asset allocation. However, armed with a good understanding of the imperfect nature of the inputs and of the sensitivity of efficient frontier analysis to changes in those inputs, it is possible to use this technique to explore the virtues, defects, and tradeoffs of different asset allocation strategies. For example, it is possible to compare a current, existing portfolio with more efficient alternatives or to measure the impact on a portfolio using different assumptions of return in, for example, high-inflation or low-inflation environments.

The capital market assumptions used to construct efficient portfolios are expected to be representative on average over the long run, but actual experience will diverge significantly from these long-run expectations. Given that no particular period is average, and in light of the sensitivity of the optimization process to changes in the capital market assumptions used as inputs, it is essential to complement the efficient frontier analysis with a rigorous battery of risk analytics to assess the range of possible returns that can be expected in different market environments.

Exploring potential negative outcomes helps to set appropriate expectations for portfolio volatility and permits a more focused assessment of the ability to withstand bad outcomes. Considering adverse scenarios is also a useful decision-making tool, as it helps avoid the common mistake of making ad hoc decisions in difficult circumstances. We consider some of the main risk analytics below.

Risk Analytics

Shortfall Analysis

Endowments should not be viewed as ends in themselves. Rather, they are the means to generate a recurring and growing income stream to support the institution's operating budget, thereby helping a college or university achieve its academic objectives. It follows that the broadest definition of "investment risk" is shortfall risk—the probability of failing to generate sufficient returns to meet the endowment's ultimate objectives. Shortfall analysis examines this risk in order to compare the attractiveness of competing asset allocations.

The more demanding the return objectives—for example, an endowment spending rate of 6 percent as opposed to 4 percent—the greater the possibility that returns may fall short in some periods. This is the primary tradeoff investors must assess between risk and return. The usual advice for those whose finances depend most heavily on investment returns, those whose budgets have the least flexibility to tolerate reductions in the distributions from their portfolios, and those who receive few or no periodic additions to capital, is that they should lean toward minimizing the volatility of returns. However, this requires the potentially painful tradeoff of adopting a more conservative portfolio with a lower expected return that does not meet the institution's long-term needs. In contrast, those colleges and universities with other sources of funding, successful fundraising, stability in their investment committee membership, and a greater flexibility in their budgets can more easily absorb a short-term decline in the portfolio's value as they attempt to earn higher returns. Rather than being more conservative within their endowment, some institutions would be better positioned for the future if they kept extra liquidity outside the endowment, such as additional money in their operating cash, a line of credit, and always doing what is possible to create a continuous inflow of contributions.

Shortfall risk analysis should consider the probability of falling short of the return objective over different horizons and the potential magnitude of the shortfall in each period. This analysis should help the committee understand what percentage of the time the endowment is likely to fall short of its return objective over a 1-, 3-, 5-, and 10-year period, with the most emphasis on the longest period. We find that too much focus on bad outcomes over one year can leave committees paralyzed with fear, which causes them to choose portfolios that are too conservative. The analysis should also consider the range of possible bad outcomes and quantify the loss in each period that would result if returns fell in the bottom 5th percentile of the return distribution.

The "appropriate" threshold level of shortfall risk is highly specific to the institution, dependent not only on objective criteria dictated by financial circumstances but also on subjective views reflecting the experience, expertise, and "comfort level" of the committee. Consequently, the only answer to the question, "How much risk can we afford to incur?" is, "It depends."

Nevertheless, measures of shortfall probability do at least provide yardsticks that enable committee members to compare the investment risks of competing portfolios in a more practical context than is provided by such tools as efficient frontier analysis. A committee that rigorously assesses shortfall risk will have a more realistic understanding of its ability to weather likely storms in the financial markets. In this way, a thorough analysis of shortfall risk can prepare committee members for bad outcomes and reduce the likelihood that they will be tempted to make knee-jerk and counterproductive asset allocation changes in the wake of a crisis.

Historical Stress Tests

Shortfall analysis based on the expected probability distribution of returns over different periods is a powerful tool for reaching sound judgments on the appropriate level of an endowment's portfolio risk. Shortfall analysis is typically based on the capital market assumptions used to construct an efficient portfolio. But like any set of projections, assumed relationships can break down, resulting in extreme outcomes. Historical stress tests focus on such extreme outcomes.

Considering how sample portfolios would have performed in historical episodes of market turmoil provides a further test of portfolio robustness, as these historical episodes encapsulate a wealth of information across economic and financial indicators of how markets have actually behaved under duress. Notably, these crises illustrate how the assumptions of efficient frontier analysis can break down, and they highlight the extent to which return volatility and correlations can be unstable. When designing a policy-benchmark portfolio, it is important to assess how the targeted asset mix would have behaved during historical financial crises, such as the great financial crisis of 2007–09 and the tech bubble. Quantifying the peak-to-trough decline of the portfolio in these and other examples of severe financial-market fragility provides useful insights and a powerful reality test.

Liquidity Risk Analysis

The financial crises of 2007–09 and COVID-19 highlighted the importance of maintaining adequate portfolio liquidity to rebalance and meet capital calls. Investors commit a specified amount of money to a private capital manager when the manager is raising a new fund; this is done with the understanding that the commitment will be drawn down over time. "Capital calls" are a legally enforceable demand issued periodically by a private capital manager to fund the commitment. The crisis resulted in direct investment losses and triggered a series of events that resulted in massive liquidations, as some institutions were forced to sell assets at depressed valuations. The memories of these events have left many wary of investment strategies that are illiquid or have the potential to become illiquid in times of financial stress, and they highlight the importance of careful liquidity modeling. A few endowments, especially those following the endowment model[3] favoring a heavy allocation to illiquid investments, were particularly hard hit. As with the management of all risks, managing liquidity risk is ultimately a question of balance: Inadequate liquidity can create undesirable consequences, but excess liquidity could unnecessarily sacrifice the long-term return and diversification benefits afforded by less liquid investment strategies.

The liquidity requirements of a portfolio stem from both external and internal demands. An example of an external demand is a withdrawal to fund a capital project when its planned funding sources have dried up. Such demands are potentially large and cannot be forecast with much precision, but they should be avoided if possible. This is why we recommend a great deal of communication between finance and investment committees in order to avoid these surprises, which require unplanned selling of endowment investments at less-than-optimal times. Internal liquidity demands include capital calls from private equity investments or margin payments on derivatives. More importantly, liquidity is needed to rebalance the portfolio to achieve active allocation targets following wide market swings. In the expected risk-and-return analyses used to design efficient portfolios, a key assumption is that the portfolio is rebalanced to remain within reasonable bounds of the central policy asset allocation target. A failure to rebalance can significantly alter the risk characteristics and long-term return of the portfolio.

Liquidity risk analysis must be an integral part of determining the suitability of the endowment's investment policy. This analysis should assess portfolio liquidity, taking into account the targeted policy asset allocation, the liquidity characteristics of each asset class, and likely external and internal demands for liquidity. The liquidity risk analysis should minimize the probability of a liquidity event that impairs the ability to rebalance the portfolio or meet outflows. Liquidity risk within an endowment can also be partially addressed through reserve policies and additional cash portfolios as outlined below. Organizations with ample reserves outside the endowment can better weather return volatility within the endowment.

Finally, if an institution has a high level of debt relative to assets and less financial flexibility than is desirable, it may be prudent to consider developing a liquidity policy. This policy can be documented in the IPS and then monitored at some predetermined regular interval. This may also result in having segregated asset pools for purpose and time horizon. There is an added behavioral benefit of committees knowing that they cannot invade these pools. This type of policy and structure has been a more common development within investment committees since 2008. The

COVID-19 crisis reinforced the soundness of this approach. Even if an institution has a strong financial situation, this may be advisable at some level.

Monte Carlo Simulation

A further tool of risk analytics is a Monte Carlo simulation. "Simulation" refers to any analytical method meant to imitate a real-life system, especially when other analyses are too mathematically complex or too difficult to reproduce. A Monte Carlo simulation randomly generates values for independent variables (e.g., asset returns) over and over to create a distribution of dependent variables (e.g., spending amounts or terminal wealth).

The great value of a Monte Carlo simulation is that it provides an entire universe or distribution of outcomes (such as investment returns or endowment market values) that can then be analyzed over different time horizons. For example, efficient frontier analysis reveals that a certain asset allocation will, on average, produce a 6.7 percent return with a 9.9 percent standard deviation. A Monte Carlo simulation goes further and estimates a probability distribution of the endowment's assets at different points in the future, thus providing responses to such questions as: What is the probability that the endowment's assets will fall below $250 million at the end of 10 years? With this type of analysis, it is easier to understand the likelihood of achieving investment goals and the inherent downside risk, rather than focusing solely on a single, average, deterministic outcome.

Each of the management tools for estimating portfolio risk—efficient frontier analysis, shortfall analysis, historical stress tests, liquidity risk analysis, and Monte Carlo simulation—have their advantages and disadvantages. The best course of action is not to choose one over another but rather to develop a mosaic approach that draws on a variety of analytical tools. However risk is expressed and analyzed, it is essential that the investment committee fully understand the range of possible outcomes that can result from its investment decisions.

Nonendowment Assets

In addition to endowment assets, the broader finances of colleges and universities often encompass a number of cash pools and different types of pension assets. These assets also entail significant fiduciary responsibilities and management complexities.

Cash and Reserves

Operating cash and reserves of all types are too often lumped together and invested in the same way. A more profitable, less risky approach is to divide such funds into several "buckets" or pools, depending on the appropriate time horizons for when these funds will be utilized or spent. The right number of buckets for an institution will depend on the amount of cash or reserves accumulated and the different needs or ultimate uses for those funds. The goal—as with good pension fund management—is to properly match assets (investments) with their associated liabilities (when the money will be spent). For example, institutions can segment their operating assets into three categories: liquidity (for daily use); contingency (seldom used); and core (rarely, if ever, used). Keeping too much in low-yielding, highly liquid funds (cash and cash equivalents) may mean that institutions are forfeiting the potential to earn higher yields.

Creating different pools enables a college or university to appropriately invest each pool, consistent with its time horizon, in a manner that will enhance returns without incurring inappropriate risks by stretching for yield.

Planned Giving Assets

The terms "planned gifts" or "planned giving assets" refer to irrevocable gifts that provide an income stream to a beneficiary, usually until his or her death, at which time the principal becomes available for the institution's use. Examples include gift annuities, pooled income funds, and charitable remainder trusts.

Planned giving assets are specialized instruments governed by numerous and complex state and federal regulations. Both administrative and investment tasks require special attention and expert handling. These investments are increasingly overseen by the investment committee due to the growing size of the portfolios. They are often managed and administered by outsourced providers. Planned giving programs focused on securing planned and estate gifts are an important way to build endowments.

Pension Plans

Virtually all colleges and universities offer some sort of retirement plan. Defined contribution 403(b) plans are the norm and are similar to the for-profit sector's 401(k) plans.

Defined benefit plans, by contrast, clearly define the monthly retirement benefit for participants through a predetermined formula that typically is based on the number of years of service and salary level, and the institution bears all the investment risk.

In both types of plans, the sponsoring institution has a fiduciary obligation to the participants. Some officials think that adopting a 403(b) plan relieves them of their fiduciary duties because the participants are choosing their own investments. This is not so. Sponsors of 403(b) plans are responsible for selecting the providers and the specific funds available to their employees, and for managing the costs incurred in administering the plans. To fulfill these fiduciary responsibilities, the institution must demonstrate that it engaged in an appropriate selection and monitoring process. Evaluating the suitability and performance of the available investment options then becomes an ongoing responsibility.

In making decisions regarding the management of defined contribution pensions, college and university officials should ask these questions:

- Have all decisions been clearly made in the best interests of plan participants?
- Does the plan follow best practices in all decisions?
- Were appropriate, documented processes followed in making all decisions related to the plan?
- Are appropriate officials regularly monitoring and evaluating the investment options available to employees?
- Given that the average active mutual fund underperforms its benchmark, are index funds available to plan participants?

Failing to address these issues carries reputational and financial risk.

Summary

The aim of designing an endowment portfolio is to determine the asset mix on the efficient frontier representing an optimal tradeoff between risk and return that maximizes the probability of achieving the endowment's long-run investment objective at an appropriate level of risk.

The asset allocation review process to design this portfolio begins with the determination of return, risk, and correlation estimates for all asset classes. Using these capital market inputs, an efficient frontier of diversified portfolios is defined using an optimization process that identifies the mix of asset classes that maximizes expected return at each level of risk. The final step in the process is to select an asset mix from the efficient frontier that is consistent with the endowment's investment objectives and constraints—that is, one that delivers the desired level of expected return at the lowest level of risk, assuming an environment with equilibrium over the long term. This portfolio must then be subjected to a rigorous risk assessment to validate the suitability of the asset mix selected and to prepare committee members and other stakeholders for possible bad outcomes.

In addition to the endowment portfolio, colleges and universities have a variety of cash and intermediate-term pools. As in the case of the endowment, each of these pools should have written investment policies governing their operations and an oversight structure so that their performance against clearly defined benchmarks is monitored on a regular basis.

Institutions also bear a fiduciary responsibility for the retirement plans they sponsor, and they must ensure that these plans provide suitable investment alternatives for beneficiaries at reasonable cost.

Once an asset allocation policy for each endowment and non-endowment pool has been established, the next step is to hire external money managers to implement the policies. Many institutions fall short in implementing this important step and fail to incorporate the same level of rigor and analysis in decisions about hiring and firing managers that they used in designing asset allocation policies. Chapter 6 outlines best practices for such decisions.

Key Questions for Boards

1. Has the investment committee largely focused on designing—and adhering to—an optimal asset allocation policy?
2. How has the committee determined that the asset mix is appropriate given the endowment's return objectives and tolerance for risk?
3. How does the committee assess whether the endowment portfolio has the appropriate level of alternative investments given the institution's situation?
4. Has the committee established a reasonable liquidity policy? How frequently is this reviewed?
5. How does the committee ensure that it has access to the necessary investment expertise to effectively incorporate alternative investments into the endowment?
6. Are investment policies in place for all managed assets, including cash, planned giving assets, reserves, and pension plans? Is the accountability for these assets clear?
7. Does the committee monitor investment-performance figures (and appropriate benchmarks) for these other managed assets? Has the appropriate oversight group reviewed these figures? If so, has the investment performance been satisfactory?
8. What processes has the committee implemented to ensure all decisions related to non-endowment assets have been made in a manner compatible with the institution's fiduciary responsibilities?

Chapter 6

Hiring Endowment-Management Professionals (Internally or Externally)

Boards and investment committees hire a broad range of investment professionals to implement the investment function: outside consultants, OCIO firms, internal staff, and investment managers. Selecting the right team for each role is a time-consuming and complex undertaking. Mistakes can be very costly and arise from a number of common behaviors. This chapter considers how to avoid frequent pitfalls of hiring and firing decisions.

The method of hiring investment professionals may vary somewhat, depending on the investment model a committee chooses to follow, but same broad principles apply.

To avoid costly turnover, a thorough search and careful selection process aimed at identifying qualities that foster an enduring relationship is essential. This requires a well-defined search process and framework, careful analysis, and thoughtful decision-making.

The key to finding the right partners is knowing what questions to ask, which we outline below. Once the hiring decision is made, it is important to be crystal clear regarding accountability and authority.

Key Factors

When evaluating prospective internal CIOs, consultants, OCIOs, and investment managers, we have found that there are six primary considerations:

Experience
Does the individual or company have long-standing experience in doing exactly what the committee wishes to have done, as opposed to being a new entrant in the field or category? If the committee wishes to hire a new firm, members should devote extra scrutiny to its activities and/or be familiar with the firm's leaders and key decision-makers.

Philosophy
It is important that the person or entity being hired share the same investment philosophy (or worldview) as the committee. There are schools of thought in investing that are difficult to reconcile, and partisans of each are likely to clash in unhelpful ways. Potential differences include:

- The belief that endowments should invest primarily in less-liquid alternative investments to maximize the illiquidity premium versus a more modest allocation to alternatives that seeks to preserve the flexibility of having greater liquidity in the portfolio. The illiquidity premium is the additional return premium that can be obtained in illiquid investments when compared to liquid investments.
- Active management versus indexing.
- A focus on managing the total portfolio risk versus a focus on hiring only "best of breed" managers, with little attention to the risk of unintended concentrated risk exposures across managers.

Process

Exactly how is the manager's investment philosophy or strategy implemented? In other words, how is the portfolio actually constructed? What analytical tools are used? Who generates the ideas? Who makes the decisions? Who implements them? Does the process seem compatible with available human resources and systems? Has the process remained consistent over time? How has it evolved?

People

Investment success is heavily dependent on the quality of the people involved. Good due diligence examines and uncovers as much as possible about the individuals involved—their education, experience, character, integrity, collegiality, competence, special skills, length of tenure at the institution or firm, and specific responsibilities.

Alignment

Be alert to conflicts of interest. With an outside company, is it motivated to make the best decisions for clients or is the focus on directing endowment assets to strategies to boost the firm's earnings? Be wary of a fee schedule that charges lower fees for advice on liquid categories and higher ones to advise on alternative investments, thus creating an inherent conflict of interest. When evaluating institutions that offer both OCIO and consulting models, request sample holdings-level reports from clients of each. Do the managers, implementation, allocation to active versus passive strategies, or other allocations vary widely between the service offerings? If so, why? Be wary of OCIO firms that direct investments toward their own proprietary vehicles, as these may have hidden costs not captured by the OCIO fee schedule. Fees must be transparent and structured in a way that aligns the interests of the endowment and the firm.

Performance

It can be difficult to determine skill by looking at returns alone. The committee should gather as much performance history as possible and examine it in rolling three- and/or five-year periods against the relevant benchmarks in order to assess the factors driving performance over time and across different market cycles. Consistency is key. If one year shows spectacular results relative to others, the committee should request further information about that year. It is also critical to assess the factors driving performance over time and across different market cycles. Are these factors consistent with the manager's stated strategy? Are the process and sources of return repeatable over time? The past track record must be carefully parsed to determine the prospects for solid risk-adjusted returns from the manager in the future.

How the Measurement Period Can Dominate Performance Histories

Howard Marks, the successful investor and former chair of the University of Pennsylvania's investment committee, writes brilliant letters that are available on his website. We cite one of them in Appendix B, but most of his letters are well worth reading. In one, he humbly outlines his experience as chair and notes that if he had started two years before he did, he would have been "considered a very average chairman . . . at best." He continues, "The principal lesson of this tale is the observation that investment timing is imprecise and difficult but extremely significant in terms of outcomes. The bottom line: Be understanding when evaluating track records, and refuse to accept the results at first glance."

When evaluating the performance of an OCIO or consultant, carefully examine the extent of discretion over other clients' portfolios. For an OCIO with discretion, determining performance is simpler than for investment consultants that do not have final discretionary authority for the decisions made. Committee members should require actual client results (with client names removed for privacy) and ask for all clients in a given category to avoid cherry picking. For example, a $200 million endowment should ask for all discretionary clients with investments of between $100 million and $500 million, along with asset allocation information and the client's actual benchmark. If information is presented regarding numerous clients, look at differences or dispersion in relative and absolute results and ask for more information if there is significant dispersion. "Simulated" or "model" returns can be misleading; they do not represent real client results and are often inflated.

When evaluating the performance of a CIO candidate, research and evaluate his or her previous investment office. It is important to confirm whether a record of success is due to the candidate's skill or that of colleagues.

Secondary Factors

A number of additional factors may be helpful for investment committee members as they assess prospective advisors, consultants, and OCIOs:

Growth plans

Are firms under consideration asset managers/advisors or asset gatherers? Firms with huge growth engines usually are less skilled at maintaining high alpha levels (the difference between a portfolio's actual returns and the return of its relevant benchmark). Committee members should ask for a history of the firm's growth over the last five years and a growth plan in assets, but also in organizational capabilities, for the next five. How does the firm plan to manage growth?

Fees

Fees are important, but fee data are often misleading. Some firms use aggressive pricing tactics in responding to a request for proposal (RFP), only to reveal actual, and much higher, fees later. These tactics are especially common when they place client assets in their own products, generating another layer of company revenue that can be difficult to uncover. Committee members should always review total fees—including both advisory fees and assumed manager fees—for two asset allocations: current and recommended. Committee members should not hesitate to demand that all fees be included, including fund-of-funds fees and any underlying manager fees, even if they are netted out of the returns of the vehicle. Increasingly, fund-of-funds fees are included but not the fees of the underlying managers within the fund-of-funds. If a firm under consideration does not include all levels of fees until the final presentation, it is guilty of questionable practices, and the investment committee should consider excluding it from further consideration. The expenses incurred with funds managed by OCIOs who bundle client assets so that all clients get the same investment-manager team (e.g., the audit, custodian, and administrative fees) are often not disclosed separately, because they are small and subtracted from fund performance. Nevertheless, the committee should ask what they are in order to compare them accurately across firms.

Open Architecture[4]

If the firm is a manager-of-managers, does it select managers from around the globe whom they deem to be the best fit for a portfolio's mandate? Alternatively, does it earn additional revenue by allocating investments to internal products? Some firms have handled these conflicts in reasonable ways and some have not. In any case, understanding their incentives is key. Asking for ways the firm can earn additional revenue in handling the institution's assets is an important question. If the firm has multiple businesses, understand how the other areas earn money and determine if personnel in any of the other areas can ask the division the committee is working with to generate revenue for the other business. Proprietary vehicles and products from which the offering firm generates additional revenue may not be disclosed in a transparent fashion—brokerage and trading are common culprits.

Service Team

What is the service model? Have committee members asked the team to indicate who will be the key contact of the investment committee, participating in each quarterly meeting? Does the person have the experience and personality to be an effective communicator? How deep are the resources behind this person in the investment and operational areas? What is the experience of those who will ultimately make and implement investment decisions? It matters if you trust the team and enjoy its company. Do you really want to work with these people?

Centralized Investment Process/Decentralized Decision-Making

Does the team assigned to work with the committee determine the investment recommendations or are they determined centrally by the firm? If the former, you could, for example, have consultants recommending an overweight to emerging markets and others from the same firm recommending an underweight to emerging markets. Either way, it is vital to obtain the track records and examine the capabilities of the people actually making investment decisions for clients' portfolios. If the firm in question is very reliant on an investment star, it is riskier to the institution for a number of reasons, including the fact that an individual's departure might bring about unwanted changes.

Dedication to the Business

What is the firm known for? If it is not for the type of service the committee is seeking, the committee should proceed with caution. If the firm has multiple businesses, it may or may not utilize the same investment manager and research teams across business units. The committee should understand the resources that are dedicated to each business. How does implementation differ in the firm's own business lines? For example, does the consulting practice use one set of managers and the OCIO business another? If so, why?

Customized Asset Allocation

Does the firm offer a single, one-size-fits-all vehicle, or does it allow tailored investment policies to reflect the particular objectives and sensitivities of the college or university?

Mission-Related Investing and Other Customization

If the implementation of sustainable investment policies (SRI/ESG) is a priority, then it is important to determine whether the firm is capable of the required customization. If an SRI/ESG portfolio is desired and you wish to make significant changes to the portfolio due to the strategies you seek to employ, it is advised that you ask the firm how they will optimize the portfolio given your specific mandate.

Operational/Back-Office Support

This is becoming increasingly important for the completion of the administrative work associated with managing portfolios. A firm's ability to handle capital calls, audit requests, tax support, cash movements, regulatory filings, financial-statement preparation, reporting, coordination with the custodian, paying investment manager fees, and negotiation of manager contracts should be explicitly understood.

Implementation

Are there investment-worthy building blocks at the asset-category level? Can the firm implement separate accounts with all of the managers with which they would like the institution to invest? How are legacy managers handled? It is very important that a committee determine which implementation model will be best for the institution. For endowments under $250 million, a "mass customization" model is likely to be the best one, as it allows the institution to benefit from preferred investment manager relationships that might otherwise be unavailable.

Capacity-Constrained Managers

How does the firm make sure all clients are treated fairly? What if the committee now has an investment allocation to a manager to which the firm doesn't have access? What happens then?

Deciding Which Model Is Right for Your Committee: The Hiring Process for Consultants, OCIOs, and Internal CIOs

An investment committee should begin the process of deciding on a particular model by reviewing members' objectives for the portfolio, as agreed to by the board. Next, the committee should review the description of key duties and responsibilities as set forth in the investment policy statement. It is often a good idea for the committee to conduct a detailed self-assessment as part of this strategic review in order to confirm that the roles and responsibilities it is tasked with fulfilling have been completed or can be done effectively by the group in place. If a self-assessment still leaves some questions unanswered, the committee may consider engaging a strategic advisor or OCIO consultant—with no ties to any particular firms or approach—who can guide it through a strategic process to determine the optimal role of the committee.

For committees deciding among the various models for endowment management, inviting several institutional peers and practitioners to address the committee in broad terms—without sales pitches—may help to clarify the most appropriate path.

In general, there is a growing movement toward issuing a request for information (RFI) and distributing it to a wide audience. An RFI should be brief and contain a few questions, the answers to which may assist the committee in deciding which attributes in an investment partner are most important. Once these attributes are identified, an RFP to a much smaller audience should then follow. An RFP response can be more than 90 pages long; if the investment committee or vice president for finance has to review 15 of them, much time will be wasted. The Greenwich Roundtable has released a thoughtful paper, *Best Governance Practices in Delegation and Consultant Selection for Long-Term Funds*, which includes a solid sample RFP.

If the organization wishes to hire an internal CIO, meeting with several key search firms who have expertise in helping institutions fill these positions is often the best approach. They can provide valuable and realistic guidance concerning compensation, requirements, and how to structure this job for success.

Finding the right CIO or OCIO is vital to the success of an endowment. A one-hour interview with a set of finalists is not enough. For a CIO candidate, multiple rounds of interviews are appropriate. For an OCIO, at least two detailed, in-person meetings—one of which should be part of a visit to the candidate's office—are recommended in order to appropriately assess capabilities, resources, and chemistry.

Finally, several reference checks are necessary to gain a sense of the experience of other clients with that firm or person. Remember that these are invariably positively skewed, so spend some time thinking about questions that will help committee members get to the heart of any particular concerns.

Manager Selection

Traditional Approach

Managers are usually hired based largely on three key factors: strong recent performance, strong recent performance, and strong recent performance. Occasionally, investment committee members will also recommend friends or neighbors or a wealthy investment professional in the hopes of obtaining a big donation from that individual, but that is emphatically not a good reason to hire that individual as a manager.

A consultant-led process does not work as well as hoped in many cases. The process typically puts most of the control of the process of selecting the manager in the hands of the consultant and all of the responsibility for the decision in the hands of the committee. Often, the process amounts to an exercise of checking off boxes to identify, for example, a small-cap value U.S. equity manager to replace one that has underperformed. The consultant proposes to the committee a few finalists who fill the bill (often because of strong recent returns) in a process often likened to a beauty contest since it provides the committee with only a superficial impression of the managers, gleaned through a brief presentation squeezed in among other committee business. Usually the manager with the best three-year track record will get the job.

As a result, many institutions find that consulting firms are of little help in the search process. Experience has taught the firms that virtually no committee will hire a manager who has performed poorly in recent periods, so they simply do not bring them to the committee's attention. One prominent consulting firm acknowledges this: "When asked to conduct a manager search, our consultants still feel pressured by investment committees to draw up lists dominated by managers with stellar recent records." We firmly believe that those who use a consultant to conduct searches for managers could improve their results significantly by giving the consultant this contrarian assignment: "Bring me three managers in which you have great confidence, but which have underperformed for the past two to three years."

Most committee members know and remember little about the managers they hire except that the firm has recently generated "good" performance. This is not surprising, given that investment committees generally conduct about an hour or so of due diligence on prospective managers. Subsequent monitoring is also very limited, because committees usually meet only three to four times a year for a few hours and even then may only review those managers with poor results.

Underperformance is the result of this unfortunate approach to hiring managers. Why? Numerous studies have shown that recent performance is a poor predictor of future performance.

The most comprehensive direct analysis of institutional investors' decisions regarding managers is a 2008 *Journal of Finance* article by Amit Goyal and Sunil Wahal called, "The Selection and Termination of Investment Management Firms by Plan Sponsors." They found evidence of return-chasing behavior and concluded that "plan sponsors have no timing ability." Managers were hired after a period of outperformance to replace others who had recently underperformed. Combining the returns of fired managers with those hired to replace them, the study found that the average transition in managers destroyed value. In addition to the opportunity costs of ill-advised turnover, these transitions entail significant transaction costs and consume the time of staff and committee members.

Market cycles don't last forever. Newly hired managers (most of whom have had recent strong performance) eventually will enter a period in which their particular style, strategy, or preferred habitat go out of favor. When that manager then experiences a period of underperformance, as do even the best managers, the investment committee knows one thing: It hired that manager because he or she had great performance and—darn it—now doesn't have it anymore. The committee often knows relatively little about the manager's philosophy, style, process, drivers of returns, or personnel. In short, committee members do not know the manager well enough to have the confidence necessary to stick with the manager through tough times.

Although there are few guarantees in the investment world, repeatedly hiring managers after periods of strong performance and then firing them after periods of weak performance is guaranteed to produce poor results. So, what can be done to prevent this behavior from continuing?

Many institutions have looked at different approaches, such as hiring internal CIOs or OCIOs, to get the committees out of searching for managers themselves, because they have seen this cycle repeated over and over, destroying hard-earned capital. However, not all CIOs and OCIOs are stellar in this regard because of limited experience; an inquiry about their approach to selecting managers should be a prominent part of any search process.

Best-Practices Approach

If a committee chooses to hire managers directly, then a better approach to the potentially flawed one described previously can be implemented by considering the following six factors:

Motivation. The motivation for initiating a search for a manager should be to fulfill a specific investment-policy or asset-class objective. Adhering to this discipline helps reduce the temptation to hire a manager simply because of great performance numbers. From time to time, stellar managers may come to the committee with an opportunistic portfolio or idea that may be advantageous, but it must be sized appropriately.

Objectives. If the motivation for seeking a manager is sound, the next step should be the establishment of clear and reasonable objectives. Specifically, what is the institution trying to accomplish with this hire? A reasonable objective might be to hire a trustworthy manager dedicated to managing mid-cap equities who is likely—over the long term—to outperform the Russell Mid-Cap Index after fees, while incurring volatility similar to that of the index.

The search then should target a solid manager who will meet these objectives, rather than attempt the impossible task of hiring "the best" manager. The best manager is simply unknowable in advance, and the quest for such a manager often deteriorates into a search for the manager with the best recent performance—a likely recipe for disappointment.

Delegation. Who should be responsible for performing due diligence on prospective managers? The process cannot be adequately accomplished by investment committee members, who serve part-time and as volunteers, no matter how smart or dedicated they may be. The process is simply too time-consuming and requires too broad a skill set. Further, committee members have more important strategic responsibilities and should not lose focus by being drawn into the weeds of portfolio management. A best-practices approach dictates that the responsibility—and accountability—for manager selection should be delegated to a full-time, professional investment staff or to an OCIO who has significant experience in the process.

Initial Screening. Establish relevant, non-performance-based criteria prior to the search, and screen out managers who do not meet those criteria, no matter how attractive their recent performance. To prevent the committee from being unduly swayed by recent performance, it might even be wise not to provide recent returns in the first round of conversations.

Relationship. Nothing improves the manager selection process more than having a professional relationship and history with a manager. If possible, the committee should hire managers with whom they have previously invested or whom they have known professionally and followed for years. Many hours, even weeks, of due diligence are no substitute for having observed a manager over several years, read the manager's quarterly reports, and followed the progress of the firm. This accumulated firsthand knowledge frees committees from relying on a manager's current marketing pitch. This knowledge also brings with it the confidence and trust necessary to stick with a manager through the inevitable tough times.

If no committee members know such a manager, seek recommendations from trusted colleagues or consultants. Use their history with, and firsthand knowledge of, managers to your advantage. The worst course of action is probably the one most widely used: selecting top-performing managers from a database.

Due Diligence. The final step of a best practice in selecting a manager is performing sound due diligence. Many institutional investors jump right into this activity, either directly or via a consultant, while overlooking the first five steps of the hiring process listed above. This is a mistake. Strong due diligence is difficult to accomplish—and probably insufficient for success—if a college or university skips or violates the preceding guidelines.

Due-diligence efforts should include comprehensive research and analysis concerning both quantitative and qualitative factors, and should encompass both investment and operational due diligence. This should entail multiple visits with the manager over several months, including one or more visits to the firm's offices, as noted above. Both reference and background checks should be conducted. Due diligence seeks information on characteristics that often are grouped into four main categories: people, philosophy, process, and performance.

Hire managers for the right reasons: a consistent process, a well-thought-through philosophy, a stable team with adequate resources for the mandate, and verification—over long periods of time and various market cycles—that the process works. Be clear that if the manager sticks to its process, but underperforms in the first three years, the committee will not abandon it. If the committee cannot make this commitment, it should reconsider whether it has the required confidence in the manager or is simply hiring based on recent performance.

Understand key reasons for hiring the manager, and identify and document at the time of hiring what may lead to eventual termination. For example, if the strategy depends on a key person, document the actions that need to be taken if that person leaves. Another important consideration is the size of allocations. If a firm increases allocations more than is appropriate for the strategy, it should be terminated. The size threshold should also be documented and the manager required to inform the committee if the threshold is surpassed. In addition, require the manager to communicate specific key personnel changes or growth.

A caveat. No matter how much time is spent on due diligence in selecting managers, the results are never perfect or foolproof, which underscores the need for diversification in the portfolio and appropriate sizing of each active decision. Even the firm that may seem to have the best strategy or personnel may succumb to a monumental surprise in poor returns, a key personnel departure, or a compliance violation that forces them out of business. Investment committee members sometimes expect the results of due diligence to "prove" who will be the superior manager—a naive and unrealistic expectation. Sound judgment of the person conducting the due diligence is an important part of the process. Many experienced investment officers who refused to make an investment after months of due diligence have dodged poor investments—not because of any specific, objective fact, but because something did not seem or feel quite right. Sound judgment or intuition is extremely valuable, but it is nearly impossible to quantify and therefore may be undervalued. Investment officers should be free to reject an investment because "it doesn't feel right." Good judgment is not a substitute for thorough analysis and careful due diligence, of course, but rather a necessary and valuable complement to it.

Firing Managers

Terminating managers is expensive, both in terms of time and portfolio turnover costs. It is common for institutions to become caught in a cycle of ill-advised replacement of managers, spending their hoped-for increased returns in turnover costs and staff time.

Institutions fall prey to several common pitfalls when terminating managers. Chief among them is impatience, resulting in overreaction to short-term underperformance. This impatience stems in part from inadequate attention to analyzing the main drivers of returns at the time of manager selection. Managers selected largely based on a track record of performance are more likely to be terminated prematurely when performance falls short. There is also a tendency to engage in episodic governance, with the timing of decisions dictated by the calendar of quarterly investment committee meetings. Rigid rules, typically based on the magnitude and duration of underperformance, reinforce the tendency to base decisions too narrowly on recent relative performance.

So when *should* a manager be fired? A manager should be fired when the investment committee has lost confidence in the individual's or firm's future ability to meet the specific endowment objectives. Investors who do not know their managers very well can lose confidence in them quickly, usually following a relatively short period of disappointing returns. Well-informed investors who trust their managers are not shaken by poor short-term performance alone. In fact, they probably understand the reasons for it, even before talking to the manager.

Legitimate reasons for reassessing confidence in a manager include:

- The loss of a key person or significant personnel turnover;
- Evidence that poor performance reflects an absence of skill or ineffective strategy;
- A material change in the manager's philosophy, process, strategy, or approach;
- A change in ownership;
- Large growth or decline in assets under management; and/or
- A deterioration in internal controls or the manager's culture of compliance.

It is, of course, also legitimate to terminate a manager whose strategy no longer fits well with the structure of the endowment's portfolio as a result of changes in asset allocations or opportunities present in the asset class they manage.

Knowing when to terminate a manager is indeed a difficult task. There is no doubt, however, that the better the committee members know their managers when they hire them, the less likely they are to fire them for the wrong reason.

Indexing

A great deal of research highlights the astoundingly high percentage of managers who underperform their benchmarks over 10-year periods. This is even more astonishing given that many funds cease operations before they make it to 10 years, reflecting a major survivorship bias that makes things look better than they are. Along with the behavioral issues that make it hard for investment committees to pick good managers and stay with them for the long term, there is compelling evidence that many more investors should pursue an indexing strategy for some or all of their assets. Indexing can be pursued through mutual funds or exchange-traded funds (ETFs).

Some believe that the branding of indexes as "passive" investing has been part of the problem. Members of investment committees are very likely to be high achievers, and few high achievers want to be called "passive." Yet indexing is anything but passive at the asset allocation level; a committee still must determine its tolerance for risks, long-term target asset allocations, and the approved asset-class ranges. Rather than make difficult choices among managers, committees choose index funds that will provide market returns minus modest fees, leaving time for the committee to focus on the decisions that will have the greatest impact on returns. The most important of these decisions are determining an institution's ability to take risks and choosing the appropriate long-term asset allocation policy.

There are many other good reasons to consider indexing. It might be advisable if the endowment's staff and investment committee lack the resources to undertake a rigorous manager-selection process and have not made the decision to partner with a trusted co-fiduciary that would make the decisions on managers. In this case, an indexed approach provides the committee a cost-effective means of easily gaining market exposure, freeing up its time to focus on strategic asset allocation decisions, risk management, and overall supervision. Indexing done well is preferable to a failed attempt to add value through active managers. Many experts would make the reasonable assertion that indexing has an appropriate role to play in segments of the market that are highly efficient, where the prospects for net-of-fee value added are poor. Indexing parts of the portfolio as a means of liquidity management is also an efficient means of maintaining market exposure while managing flows in and out of the endowment.

When choosing an indexed fund manager, committees should consider which one has the tightest tracking error relative to the benchmark and offers competitive fees, low trading costs, and convenience. Some nuanced indexed approaches cause performance to follow the returns of the benchmark less closely. Even though an indexed approach simplifies matters, choosing the right partner and ensuring proper implementation still require close attention.

Summary

Managing a large, multi-asset-class portfolio is a complex task that requires a broad mix of skills, powerful analytical tools, and a finely honed process. Developing the right mix of internal and external capabilities to effectively undertake this endeavor requires astute hiring decisions that dodge common pitfalls. The time spent assembling a strong team of internal and external resources, however, can pay off in better returns and lower risk. This chapter has set out the key principles to follow in selecting an investment team.

Key Questions for Boards

1. What has the investment committee done to ensure that the group follows a rigorous investment and operational due-diligence process in hiring and firing investment managers? Has this process been documented?

2. What does the committee do to avoid falling prey to such common pitfalls as return chasing, impatience, episodic governance, and rigid decision-making rules?

3. What has the committee done best? Where has the committee failed to add value? Has the committee measured the cumulative impact of manager selection on the market value of the institution's endowment over the past 10 years?

4. Has the committee undertaken a strategic exercise to determine which model of investment (consulting, OCIO, CIO) will be best for the institution? How frequently will the committee revisit this decision?

5. How frequently do committee members weigh the merits of using indexed approaches to manage all or part of the portfolio?

Chapter 7

Risk Management

Fiduciaries must be aware of the risks inherent in all of their investment decisions. Throughout this book, we have addressed the issues of measuring and managing risk in order to emphasize that such actions must be integral to all aspects of portfolio management. Given the topic's importance and complexity, this chapter brings together some of the key insights in one place and explores other non-investment risks that must be taken into account.

Since the Great Recession and bear market of 2008–2009, most investment committee members have realized the importance of practicing risk management throughout the portfolio construction process. This realization reversed what had become an over-reliance on generating returns, and has led to the development of greater sophistication in the research and practice of risk-management techniques.

In reality, only a select few investment committees are able to endure large investment losses without succumbing to the temptation of selling into the trough. Such knee-jerk reactions to adversity compound the misfortune of the sharp market decline by depriving the endowment of the possibility of participating in subsequent rallies.

Identifying "Risk Tolerance"

Assessing risks is not intuitive. All decisions made in uncertainty are hard, but decisions on how to measure uncertainty and how much to accept are harder still. Experienced committee members know that while identifying risk tolerance can be difficult as an individual, it is even more challenging to a group. Committees are composed of multiple individuals with varying biases, objectives, and experience, and they may not know each other well. Sometimes the group may adopt the view of the member with the highest tolerance for risk, and sometimes the lowest, or it may veer wildly between the two. This may result in the costly practice of increasing risk when markets are performing strongly and are at their most expensive, and reducing it after a period of disappointing returns. Although many members of investment committees do not feel that their institution is at risk for this behavior, it has happened at many institutions.

In addition to having different appetites for risk, committee members may differ in the measures of risk that resonate most with them. It is therefore important to express risk in a variety of ways and to couch those measurements in terms of variables that matter most to the institution. Discussion about the probability that an endowment will sustain a catastrophic loss, or generate a consistently negative return such that the spending distribution erodes the value of the endowment significantly over a long period, is likely to resonate more effectively than discussion of abstract or statistical concepts such as standard deviation. Scenarios illustrating how a portfolio would perform in a variety of market conditions, including severe financial crises, can be effective tools to communicate the concept of risk. Concrete examples of poor outcomes that can be expected from different asset allocation policies can help committee members reach judgments about both the capacity and the willingness to assume risk.

As we have emphasized throughout this book, an endowment's risk and return targets should be aligned with the spending policy, broader finances, and strategic direction of the institution. Those assisting an investment committee in achieving its goals need to ask searching questions that inform the institution's ability to withstand absolute return volatility, an important risk for a college or university. These include questions about the institution's financial situation, which includes sources of the operating budget, the competitive strength of the institution, current financial resources relative to outstanding debt, and future capital plans and needs. Taken together, these factors provide an insight into the institution's financial resilience and ability to withstand a sharp decline in asset value.

The difficulty of identifying tolerance for risk is compounded by the wide range of risks inherent in investment management. As we saw in chapter 3, investing to meet a return objective necessarily involves price fluctuations (market risk), possible weaknesses in the investment decision-making process (behavioral risk), potential difficulties in the sale of investments (liquidity risk), trading with others who might not fulfill their obligations (counterparty risk), losses arising from errors or fraud (operational risk), the possibility that some investments will generate adverse publicity for the investor (reputation risk), and the likelihood of misaligned incentives, either within the investor's institution or between the investor and third parties (conflict-of-interest risk). The committee must reach a judgment on how best to manage each of the various risks in attempting to meet its objective for investment returns. Some of these judgments will involve tradeoffs across different types of risk.

Obviously, too much investment risk, manifested through return variability, is a bad thing. But it can be equally costly when an institution excessively reduces risk. To be overly risk averse across the entire institution imposes serious opportunity costs that will hurt an institution in the long run. At most institutions, even the most careful measures intended to reduce costs within an operating budget will not equal the benefit of an additional 1 percent return on an endowment over time. This problem is especially acute when the investment committee acts in isolation from others responsible for the financial health of the college or university—particularly the finance committee—if it also operates in an overly conservative manner. Some examples of these policies include issuing only fixed-rate debt (or no debt at all), keeping unusually high levels of operating cash, etc.

This is a task so difficult that even the well-respected endowment-management teams at large universities have had difficulty grappling with it. Insufficient coordination between treasury and investment functions has led to numerous problems, including lack of necessary liquidity to make capital calls and/or payroll. We have also seen memories fade too quickly regarding financial crises, and too few institutions have learned from their mistakes—and the mistakes of others.

We hope that the picture we have painted above has gained the reader's attention, and that it will lead to profound dialogue and debate on the subject of the institution's tolerance for risk and to improved communication within the investment committee and with the board. We encourage everyone to build a more appropriate and robust enterprise risk-management framework. An investment committee should consider carefully the questions in the following section—and revisit the topic of risk formally at least once each year.

Understanding Institutional Risk

By listing the institutional risks here, we are not suggesting that the investment committee is accountable for answering all the attendant questions, but we are recommending that members be aware of other risks the institution faces that affect the organization's ability to withstand volatility in returns. For example, an institution that is facing a crisis concerning enrollment and tuition discounting, combined with a high ratio of debt to endowment assets, has a very different risk profile than one with a strong pipeline of students, pricing strength, and significant cash reserves. Committees should focus on the connection between the factors that are outside the purview of the committee, yet, in an optimal world, should inform endowment-management decisions. As we have discussed throughout this book, the work of the investment committee can't take place in a vacuum and needs to be informed by input from other committees and the administration.

If the institution has outstanding debt, the credit rating is a very simple and effective measure of the institution's ability to withstand return variability within the endowment. Read the rating agencies' reports about the factors that led to their ratings. Be aware of the variables that can harm the institution's credit rating and consider the risk of a downgrade during comprehensive committee reviews of endowment and institutional risk.

If an institution does not have outstanding debt, the following items represent a list that may be appropriate to consider in order to have a global view of the institution's risk tolerance. We recognize that each institution's situation is unique, so we provide these questions as examples of some items that may be appropriate for you to consider.

Operating Risk

If the institution's operating budget is dependent on factors that are in flux—like public funding (which is decreasing) or tuition revenue (which could also decrease because of increasing tuition-discount rates or decreases in enrollment)—the institution will become even more reliant on revenue from fundraising and the endowment. This reliance affects the institution's investment risk tolerance.

- **Operating Budget:** What is the operating budget's mix of resources? How much of the operating budget comes from the endowment? A high level leads to greater sensitivity to variability in returns. A lower level, perhaps counterintuitively, allows a much higher level of risk within the portfolio because it will have very little short-term impact. Part of risk management is managing the operating-budget mix, ideally by adding revenue sources. This is clearly a topic for strategic board engagement. Are there ways the institution can use its physical plant to add revenue?
- **Tuition Discounting/Enrollment Trends:** Are tuition-discounting trends or enrollment declines likely to increase pressure for higher endowment spending? Are there other aspects of the institution's business model that could impact spending or liquidity needs?

Financial Risk

Debt
- The ratio of debt to other financial resources is important. Does the institution have a very high level of debt (both in absolute terms and compared to the size of the endowment)? High debt relative to overall endowment size limits the ability to take risk, whereas low debt provides greater financial flexibility.
- What are fundraising forecasts? What can be done to sustain fundraising?

Liquidity
- How much of a cash cushion does the organization traditionally keep to provide liquidity? Is this the right amount given the size of the operating budget and other available liquidity (e.g., through a line of credit)?
- Are there large capital needs that have yet to be addressed that may pressure the spending-rate distribution or the endowment in total?

Investment Risk
- Is the portfolio effectively diversified?
- Is there a robust oversight process for selecting investment managers?

- How much illiquidity is there within the portfolio in current positions and in uncalled commitments, both in absolute terms and as a percentage of the portfolio?
- How much would the portfolio decline today if there were another crisis similar to the recession of 2008–2009?

Answers to these questions begin to provide a means of assessing an institution's risk management and to emphasize the types of information that an investment committee should review periodically based on the institutional risks. Other questions specific to particular institutions can be developed. Access to and analysis of such information requires open communication among board members, regardless of individual committee assignments, and encourages the communication we discuss throughout the book in order to achieve long-term investment success. We believe the board should hold regular strategic-planning sessions and should carefully document them. This information should be furnished to any new board members during orientation as well as to current board members at regular intervals.

Investment Manager Operational Risk

In managing this risk, an institution must seek to identify and investigate potential areas of operational risk involved when hiring investment managers, especially in the alternative investment area. Institutions should evaluate investment-manager controls, processes, and personnel in place to address them. Some things to evaluate include whether or not the investment managers you employ have:

- An institutional quality infrastructure that includes a robust governance structure and empowerment of the non-investment function to prevent things like fraudulent activity or inappropriate preferential treatment of trades;
- An emphasis on compliance with securities regulations;
- Segregation of duties within the trade flow process;
- An institutional and stable investor base to avoid significant redemptions that could arise with a largely retail client base; and
- Institutional quality service providers and third-party administration (i.e., not self-administration).

In order to fulfill appropriate operational due diligence, it may be appropriate to consider background checks on key people within the investment management organizations you seek to hire to help fulfill your investment function, as well as ongoing media searches on existing managers and key partners.

Other Types of Risk

- **Changing strategy at the wrong time.** Asset allocation is the most important driver of returns and must be reviewed strategically approximately every three years, but it should never be reviewed in times of extreme market volatility. While an investment policy statement should provide for certain ranges of hoped-for return in each asset class, thereby allowing for some flexibility, committees should remain within these ranges even during times of market euphoria or stress. Major changes to asset allocation policy should only occur during times of relative normality. The governing board would be wise to codify this policy well ahead of time.

- **Significantly underperforming a benchmark.** As luck would have it, the most difficult member often joins the investment committee just when things are going the worst. Sometimes change in investments is necessary, but we believe that any such change must be based on a careful analysis of the sources of poor performance and an assessment of whether the reasons for the bad outcome reflect a broken process or particular market conditions. Any change must be taken with a forward-looking perspective.

- **Peer-comparison risk.** As we highlighted previously, mimicking peers is not a sound approach to asset allocation and other investment decisions, except in the unlikely event that their circumstances closely match those of your institution. While we believe strongly that an institution's primary objective in managing an endowment must be meeting its own unique financial needs, comparing an asset allocation policy to those of peers can serve as an informative check on the policy process and its assumptions—but it should not dictate the investment policy ultimately adopted. Many investment committees are greatly influenced by peers, and few of them can tolerate significantly underperforming their peers without some action. Too often this action is ill-advised and results in abandoning an investment strategy—usually at just the wrong time!

- **Reputational risk.** Bad publicity arising from the endowment's investments can come from a variety of sources. Managers included in the endowment may be sanctioned by the SEC or another regulatory agency; asset classes in the portfolio, such as hedge funds or private equity, may fall from favor in the public eye as a result of high fees and poor performance; and investments in particular sectors, industries, or regions may appear to some to be incompatible with the institution's core values. There is significant reputational risk if there are any conflicts of interest involving committee members and any of the portfolio's investments. Some of these sources of reputational risk can be mitigated through careful investment and operational due diligence to avoid hiring managers prone to ethical lapses, lack of transparency, or outsized fees. Others can be addressed by discussing the endowment's investment rationale with a broad range of stakeholders and explaining tradeoffs that might arise between social issues and the practical exigencies of portfolio management.

- Political risk. Colleges and universities have a high public profile. Rising tuition, ballooning student debt, and increased student activism have made higher education a more politically charged arena than it has been for some time. The increased possibility of political intervention in the internal workings of colleges and universities is another form of risk of which investment committees must be aware. In the past, some politicians have begun to investigate the practices of institutions with endowments larger than $1 billion, and whether these institutions should continue to be tax-exempt. To avoid ham-fisted rules, board members and institutional presidents should engage with the political process and carefully explain the consequences of any governmental interventions.
- Sustainability Risk: Investment exposure to sustainability factors—such as environmental, social and employee matters, respect for human rights, anti-corruption, and anti-bribery—may have a positive or negative impact on the financial performance of your investments. Negative sustainability risks can also impact reputational risk and, given increasing environmental and social policy regulation, political risk. For this reason, whether or not an endowment has chosen to implement an ESG investment strategy, it is wise for the committee to understand how their managers take sustainability risk into account in the management of their individual strategies.

Summary

Evaluation and management of risk must be integral to every aspect of portfolio management. Ultimately, the art of risk management is striking the right balance across the wide range of risks inherent in investing. Avoiding risk can be as costly as taking it, and investment committees must take a holistic view of the institution's financial state in order to accurately evaluate appropriate tolerance for risk. Communication among committees, staff, senior leadership, and other stakeholders is key in order to develop a shared understanding of the tradeoffs across risks and to help prevent knee-jerk reactions to adversity.

Appendix A: Sample Investment Committee Checklist

Ultimately, the success or failure of the investment committee in fulfilling its fiduciary responsibility rests on chemistry. The committee is charged with making complex decisions with highly uncertain outcomes. Such decisions must be made with deliberation, drawing on the wise counsel and active participation of all members of the committee. Committee members must be prepared for adversity and meet setbacks without rancor or recrimination. This can only be achieved by fostering a culture of good governance within the committee. A culture of best practices comes from a shared understanding of the importance of key behaviors, which the authors have organized into five categories:

- Awareness of the endowment's mission
- Committee structure and practice
- Decision-making process
- Attitudes and biases
- Controls

I. Awareness of the Endowment's Mission

✓ The investment committee has a well-defined and thoroughly thought-out vision for the role of investments in meeting the objectives of the institution and its stakeholders and it has effectively communicated this to all investment partners.

✓ The investment objectives established by the committee are aligned with the broader institutional mission, are realistic, and are based on a comprehensive appreciation of the full range of risks—including unlikely but potentially very damaging investment outcomes.

II. Committee Structure and Practice

✓ The investment committee has the appropriate number of committee members, meets the right number of times annually, and addresses the right issues.

✓ The average tenure of the investment committee members is long enough to ensure institutional memory and continuity, while building in sufficient turnover to benefit from fresh insights.

✓ The committee focuses on policy issues and leaves implementation and operational decisions to staff/service providers (e.g., consultant/OCIO/individual specialist investment managers).

✓ The committee adequately monitors the implementation of its policy decisions.

- ✓ All committee members are sufficiently well trained and knowledgeable about investments, capital markets, and risk management to properly discharge their responsibilities. They come to meetings prepared.
- ✓ All committee members have high ethical and professional standards, disclose possible conflicts of interest, and take their fiduciary responsibilities seriously.
- ✓ The committee fosters an environment of open discussion, trust, and mutual respect. It encourages and listens attentively to constructive dissent.
- ✓ Committee members prepare for and actively participate in meetings.
- ✓ The committee reflects diverse perspectives.

III. Decision-Making Process

- ✓ The committee bases decisions on a thorough consideration of sound and objective analysis. When adequate supporting information has not been provided with enough lead time to enable thoughtful analysis, a decision is postponed.
- ✓ The committee is given a complete and balanced assessment of any potential investment action, especially when decisions are not clear-cut.
- ✓ The committee makes timely decisions, and its decisions are implemented in a timely manner.
- ✓ Members of the committee feel comfortable raising doubts about a decision if circumstances change.
- ✓ All members' views are fully aired and properly discussed before making decisions. Deliberations are open, thorough, engaging, and lively.
- ✓ The committee has established clear guidelines for the types of decisions that require its consideration and those that may be delegated to others. It periodically reviews the guidelines.
- ✓ The committee carefully plans its work schedule to ensure that all topics that must be addressed to fulfill its fiduciary responsibilities are reviewed regularly.

IV. Attitudes and Biases

- ✓ The committee has confidence in the advice it receives from investment managers and service providers. It nevertheless carefully probes the reports, analyses, and recommendations it receives.
- ✓ The committee welcomes investment policy innovation and recognizes that capital markets are evolving every day. It adopts innovations with deliberate speed.
- ✓ The committee remains disciplined and continues to strike an appropriate balance between long-term and short-term considerations, even in the face of significant investment setbacks.
- ✓ The committee's investment decisions are forward-looking and value-oriented (i.e., price-sensitive), not driven by past returns or "rules of thumb."

✓ In evaluating new investment strategies or managers, the committee focuses on process and current valuations rather than past performance.

✓ While it is aware of peers' asset allocation and performance, the committee's main focus is on setting objectives that are tailored to the institution's needs and outperforming their own policy objectives.

✓ The committee members read all of the material given to them in support of discussions and decisions and come to meetings well prepared.

V. Controls

✓ The committee has established a clear process of review and accountability.

✓ The committee sets clear expectations for the investment outcomes it is targeting and regularly reviews the results of its decisions.

✓ The committee periodically reviews investment operations to ensure that there are effective and transparent compliance systems, legal reviews, and control procedures in place.

✓ The committee reviews investment performance in the short- and long-term, relative to appropriate investable (rather than aspirational) comparators and expectations, and understands the context in which the performance is being delivered.

Source: Strategic Investment Group

Appendix B:
Suggested Reading for New Investment Committee Members

Books

Ellis, Charles D. *Investment Policy: How to Win the Loser's Game, 2nd Edition*. Burr Ridge, IL: Irwin Professional Publishing, 1992.

Ellis, Charles D. *Winning the Loser's Game, 6th Edition: Timeless Strategies for Successful Investing*. New York, NY: McGraw-Hill Education, 2013.

Eslinger, Lisa M. *Understanding Foundation Finances: Financial Oversight and Planning for Foundation Boards*. Washington, D.C.: AGB Press, 2014.

Kochard, Lawrence E. and Cathleen M. Rittereiser. *Foundation and Endowment Investing: Philosophies and Strategies of Top Investors and Institutions*. Hoboken, NJ: Wiley, 2008.

Swensen, David F. *Pioneering Portfolio Management: An Unconventional Approach to Institutional Investment*. New York, NY: Free Press, 2009.

Yoder, Jay A. *The Investment Committee*. Washington, D.C.: AGB Press, 2011.

Papers, Articles, and Other Resources

AGB Board of Directors' Statement on Conflict of Interest with Guidance on Compelling Benefit. Washington, D.C.: Association of Governing Boards of Universities and Colleges, 2013.

AGB Board of Directors' Statement on the Fiduciary Duties of Governing Board Members. Washington, D.C.: Association of Governing Boards of Universities and Colleges, 2015.

Bahlmann, David, Peter F. Campanella, and Thomas B. Heck. "The Outsourced Chief Investment Officer: A Remedy for Your Endowment's Fiduciary Fatigue." *Trusteeship*, May/June 2013, Vol. 21, No. 3, Association of Governing Boards of Universities and Colleges, Washington, D.C.

Bass, David. *Spending and Management of Endowments under UPMIFA*. Washington, D.C.: Association of Governing Boards of Universities and Colleges, 2010.

Bass, David. "Fundraising and Endowment Resilience: Lessons for Leadership." Washington, D.C.: Council for Advancement and Support of Education, 2021.

Best Governance Practices in Delegation and Consultant Selection for Long-Term Funds. Cos Cob, CT: Greenwich Roundtable, 2016.

Cabot, Walter M. "The All-Important Relationship Between the Board and Its Investment Committee"

CFA Institute: This organization publishes several excellent publications, including a guide to writing an investment policy. See cfa.org.

DeVaan, Jon. "What's in Store for Endowments?" *Trusteeship*, March/April 2017, Vol. 25, No. 2, Association of Governing Boards of Universities and Colleges, Washington, D.C.

Ellis, Charles D. "Best Practice Investment Committees." *Journal of Portfolio Management*, Winter 2011, Vol. 37, No. 2, Institutional Investor Journals, New York, NY.

Gary, Susan N. "Fiduciary Duties and ESG Investing." *Trusteeship*, November/December 2015, Vol. 23, No. 6, Association of Governing Boards of Universities and Colleges, Washington, D.C.

Gumas, John, and Robert J. Nava. "Socially Responsible Investing: Lessons from the Field." *Trusteeship*, July/August 2014, Vol. 22, No. 4, Association of Governing Boards of Universities and Colleges, Washington, D.C.

Harvard Management Company, Inc. *Annual Endowment Report*. Yearly reports are available at hmc.harvard.edu.

Moody's Investors Service: Annual reports on the state of higher education provide valuable insights on enrollment trends, cost trends, etc.

NACUBO Study of Endowments: Yearly reports are available for purchase at nacubo.org.

Strategic Investment Management, LLC. www.ocio.org. This educational resource helps existing and potential clients of OCIOs to understand and maximize the benefits of an OCIO relationship.

Yale Investments Office. *The Yale Endowment*. Yearly reports are available at investments.yale.edu.

Appendix C: Glossary of Useful Terms

1, 2, and 3 Standard Deviation Losses - Assuming a normal distribution in any given year, returns equal to or lower than these losses would be experienced with a probability of 17.0%, 2.5%, and 0.5%, respectively.

Alpha - A measure of the difference between a portfolio's actual returns and its expected performance, given its level of risk as measured by beta. A positive alpha figure indicates the portfolio has performed better than its beta would predict. For actively managed funds, this can be a sign that the manager has added value to portfolio performance. A negative alpha indicates that the portfolio has underperformed, given the expectations established by the portfolio's beta.

Alpha Confidence Interval (95%) - The range within which the true quarterly alpha of the manager is estimated to fall, with a 95% probability.

Annual Return - The annualized return of the manager or index for the period.

Annual Value Added - The value added by the manager in excess of the index.

Annualized Tracking Error - The standard deviation of the annual value added by the manager. Another indicator of how well an index fits a manager's investment style. A tracking error below 2% indicates a close fit, and above 5% indicates a loose fit.

Arbitrage Strategies - Attempt to exploit temporary price discrepancies between securities by buying the cheaper one and selling short the more expensive one. Investment managers use historical relationships between instruments in different markets to predict future trends of movements in price.

Asset Allocation - The distribution of assets among asset classes. Active asset allocation involves the overweighting or underweighting of a particular asset class relative to the target portfolio's allocation.

Asset Class - A broadly defined group of securities that have similar risk and return characteristics. For example, most large institutional investors such as endowment funds divide the universe of investable securities into the following categories (asset classes): domestic equities; international equities; domestic fixed income; global fixed income; real estate; venture capital; alternative investments/special situations; and cash and equivalents.

Batting Average vs. Index - The percentage of quarters that the manager beat the index. For example, a batting average of 60%, which is good, means that the manager beat the index in 60% of the quarters.

Benchmark - A reference market index that serves as a basis for a performance comparison and, in the case of publicly traded investments, a passive alternative to active management.

Beta - (1) A measure of a portfolio's sensitivity to market movements. By definition, the beta of the benchmark index is 1.00. A portfolio with a 1.50 beta can be expected to perform 50% better than the index in a rising market, and 50% worse in a down-market environment. (2) A risk measure derived from a regression of the manager's returns against the index's returns. For example, a beta of 1.0 means the manager's returns have been exactly as volatile as those of the index; a beta of 1.5 means the manager's returns have been 50% more volatile.

Beta, Alpha, and Portable Alpha - Beta and alpha have many meanings in statistics and finance. In the context of developing policy portfolios, beta is the market return in any given asset class; for example, the S&P 500 for U.S. equities. Alpha is the expected excess return over the market benchmark from active management. Portable alpha involves transferring alpha from asset classes where confidence in active management is high to classes where it is low, while still retaining the beta returns of the receiving class.

Beta Confidence Interval (95%) - The range within which the true beta of the manager is estimated to fall, with 95% probability.

Carried Interest - Expressed as percentage of net portfolio profits, usually 20% in the case of straight private equity, but as much as 25% or 30% in the case of venture capital.

Co-Investment - Opportunities to be made available to limited partners, usually with certain restrictions.

Composite - A combination of two or more separate portfolios. For example, by treating all individual venture capital partnerships as a single consolidated portfolio, it is then possible to calculate performance statistics for a complete venture capital program. The same technique can be applied to any combination of portfolios or indices for which consolidated results are desired.

Commitment Period - The period in years from date of final closing during which investments will be made.

Convertible Arbitrage - Strategies generally consist of the purchase (or short sale) of a company's relatively undervalued (or overvalued) convertible security, such as a convertible bond, convertible preferred stock, warrant, or an option, as well as the short sale (or purchase) of the relatively overvalued (or undervalued) underlying security for which the convertible security can be exchanged. There are a number of different styles of the strategy, but most managers aim to profit from: a) the yield return of the investments, and b) their relative volatility.

Convexity - The rate of change of duration for a given change in yield. Convexity can be positive (for an option-free bond such as a Treasury security) or negative (for a mortgage security with an embedded "short" option position). In a rising interest rate environment, prices of bonds with negative convexity will drop by a greater amount than implied by a given rise in interest rates. For example, when interest rates decline suddenly and/or sharply, prices of mortgage-backed securities typically do not rise in the same proportion as option-free Treasury bonds, since the life of a mortgage-backed security may be suddenly shortened if homeowners prepay their mortgages, thus exercising their "long" prepayment option in a new lower interest rate environment. Changes in bond price are based on a group of factors including the duration effect and the convexity effect.

Correlation - A statistical measure used to express the relationship between two variables. The sign of the correlation coefficient indicates the direction of the relationship between two variables, while the absolute value indicates the extent of the relationship.

Correlation Coefficient - A measure (ranging in value from –1 to +1) of the association between two variables. If a variable is higher than its average value at the same time as another variable is higher than its average value, two variables are said to be positively correlated. If a variable is lower than its average value at the same time as another variable is higher than its average value, the two variables are said to be negatively correlated. If there is no discernable relationship, the two variables are said to be uncorrelated. The closer the correlation coefficient is to +1, the more the two variables are positively correlated; the closer to –1, the more negatively correlated; and the closer to zero, the more uncorrelated. When considering adding an asset to a portfolio, the more it is negatively correlated or uncorrelated to the other assets in the portfolio, the greater the diversification the asset brings to the portfolio.

Covariance - The extent to which two variables "vary together," used to determine the total risk associated with interrelated investments. A positive sign indicates a direct relationship, while a negative sign indicates an inverse relationship.

Credit/Distressed - These hedge fund strategies include investments in securities of companies that are experiencing a liquidity crisis, have defaulted on their debt obligations, have filed for Chapter 11 bankruptcy protection, or are otherwise financially distressed. A variety of strategies may be employed, including long credit, short selling, and capital structure arbitrage investing.

Credit Quality - Bonds issued by corporations and non-federal-government entities are rated by agencies such as Moody's or Standard & Poor's, with ratings descending from AAA to AA to A, etc. Issues rated BBB or higher are considered to be "investment grade," while unrated or lower-rated issuers are often referred to as "high yield" or "junk" bonds. The rating agencies assign ratings to a portfolio's securities based on their judgment regarding an issuer's ability to meet its obligations. U.S. Treasury securities are considered to have the highest credit quality.

Disequilibrium Real Returns - The expected average annual real return after adjusting expected fixed-income returns to reflect current disequilibrium conditions in yields.

Duration - The effect on price of a rise or fall of 1% in interest rates. For example, if the duration of a bond is five years, a 1% rise in interest rates will result in a 5% decline in the bond's price, all else being equal. The reverse is true for a decline in rates.

Equity/Statistical Arbitrage - A hedge fund strategy that seeks to exploit temporary price disparities among assets that have historically maintained a statistically significant, stable relationship. Unlike relative value, this strategy is more dependent on technical variables than fundamental analysis.

Equity Long/Short - These hedge fund strategies invest in equities and equity derivatives both on the long and short side. Here, the outcome is somewhat more correlated with movements in financial markets. Stock selection techniques are extremely varied and utilize fundamental analysis, technical analysis, quantitative programs, macro, and/or sector approaches, among others. The focus may be on global stock markets, country- or region-specific markets, individual industries, different capitalization classes within the same market, and other asset-class bets. The manager will often have a net long bias (i.e., will generally have some market exposure).

Equity Market-Neutral - A hedge fund strategy that seeks to exploit temporary pricing anomalies. An inexpensive stock is purchased while a related expensive stock is simultaneously sold short. Many managers in this category look at fundamental variables using quantitative techniques, and try to avoid style, industry, capitalization, and other non-stock-specific exposures.

Excess Return - The annualized out-performance of the manager versus the benchmark.

Explained Variance R^2 - The fraction of total variance in the return series that is explained by the benchmark.

Fixed Income Arbitrage - A hedge fund strategy that involves purchasing one fixed-income security and simultaneously selling a similar fixed-income security. The sale of the second security is done to hedge the underlying market risk contained in the first security. Typically, the two securities are related either mathematically or economically such that they move similarly with respect to market developments. Generally, the difference in pricing between the two securities is small, and this is what the fixed-income arbitrageur hopes to gain.

General Partner - Name of the legal entity sponsoring and performing day-to-day operations of a fund organized as a limited partnership, which is often formed under Delaware or Cayman Island law.

Geographic Focus - Country or regional concentration of targeted transactions.

Global Macro - These hedge fund strategies speculate on the direction of currencies, commodities, equities, and/or bonds. They generally rely on both fundamental and technical analysis and combine long and/or short positions with leverage to optimize returns. Correlation with typical benchmarks is low except during exceptional volatility periods, when the manager might hold a directional bet in a particularly affected market (e.g., a long bet on Russian bonds when Russia defaulted).

Hurdle Rate - The rate compounded annually to be earned on capital drawn for investment or expenses before the general partner becomes entitled to carried interest.

Immunization - To create and maintain a portfolio that will have a certain return over a specified horizon, irrespective of changes in interest rates. By matching the duration of assets and liabilities, along with periodic rebalancing procedures, investors can lock in rates and minimize the reinvestment risk that occurs with a simple maturity-matching strategy. Immunization balances the impact of capital gain or loss against reinvestment risk.

Index - A number calculated by weighting several prices or rates according to a set of predetermined rules. A financial-market index is a statistical construct that measures the relative or absolute price changes and/or returns in stock, fixed-income, currencies, or futures markets. The purpose of the index calculation is usually to provide a single number whose behavior is representative of the movements of a variety of prices or rates indicative of a market. An investable index is one in which an investor can purchase securities and match the underlying market's performance, less transactions costs. For example, it is relatively easy to create an S&P 500 Index fund by purchasing all 500 stocks in the same weight as the index, but it is much more difficult to replicate certain emerging-markets indices.

Information Ratio - A measure of the likelihood that superior performance is the result of superior knowledge or judgment by an investment manager. The average excess return over benchmark (usually referred to as alpha) divided by its standard deviation.

Kurtosis - A measure of whether a distribution is more or less "peaked" than a normal distribution (and for this reason sometimes called "excess kurtosis"). Higher kurtosis means that more of the variance is due to infrequent extreme deviations (positive or negative) as opposed to frequent modest-sized deviations. The normal distribution has a kurtosis of zero. Thus, a positive kurtosis implies that the fund is more likely than predicted by the normal distribution to have large positive or negative return months, more commonly known as "fat tails."

Leverage - The degree of indebtedness used to finance investment activity. For example, a leverage ratio of 2:1 indicates that $2 is borrowed against each $1 invested. Since leveraging enhances both positive and negative returns, it increases volatility but also profit potential.

Liquidity Premium - An extra component of yield or return required to compensate the investor for the possibility that an adequate resale market may not develop for a security.

Liquidity Score - A weighted average of the liquidity score of underlying assets. The liquidity scores for assets range from 0% for private equity to 100% for cash and represent an estimate of the percentage of assets that could be liquidated in one month without material market impact.

Management Fee - Expressed in basis points (100 basis points = 1%) of committed capital during the investment period and of invested capital during the liquidation phase.

Manager - Name of the legal entity managing the fund.

Manager Performance - The value added by the investment manager relative to an appropriate benchmark that reflects the manager's investment style. For example, although the entire U.S. equity sector is measured against the Dow Jones Wilshire 5000 Index, one can measure the individual managers against other benchmarks, such as the Russell 2000 (a small-cap index) or the S&P 500 equal-weighted index (a mid-cap benchmark).

Manager Structure - The value added by the manager when it chooses a portfolio structure that differs from the portfolio structure of the asset-class benchmark. For example, in U.S. equities this is the value added by selecting managers that focus on small- or mid-cap stocks, when the benchmark for the asset class (i.e., the Dow Jones Wilshire 5000) has a much higher weighting to large cap growth stocks and less exposure to small-cap and mid-cap stocks.

Margin Purchase - Use of money borrowed from a broker/dealer to purchase securities.

Minimum Commitment - The minimum amount of capital commitment accepted from each limited partner.

Net Asset Value (NAV) - The value of the investment pool, calculated by taking the market value of all securities held in the portfolio and dividing it by the total number of shares or units outstanding.

Net Long/Net Short - Exposure occurs when a manager has more long exposure than short exposure. For example, if a portfolio is 100% long and 25% short, we say the manager is 75% net long. Conversely, if a portfolio is 100% long and 110% short, we say the manager is 10% net short.

Nominal Return - The expected average annual return of the portfolio before adjusting for inflation.

Nominal Tax Efficiency - Estimates the percentage of pre-tax nominal returns that an investor could expect to retain after subtracting taxes.

Objective - Target Internal Rate of Return (IRR), stated in specific terms but with appropriate qualifiers.

Observations - The number of quarters used in the computations.

Policy Portfolio - A long-term investment strategy that should achieve the objectives of the institution, provided markets deliver equilibrium returns consistent with the assumed rates of return for the asset classes selected for investment. The portfolio consists of a definition of each allowable asset class, a benchmark index for each asset class and the total portfolio, a strategic asset allocation, and a set of risk-control ranges.

Portable Alpha - Portable alpha involves transferring alpha from asset classes in which an investor believes there is a greater opportunity to create positive alpha to classes in which the opportunity is low, while still retaining the beta returns of the receiving class.

Quarterly Alpha - The quarterly excess return of the manager, as estimated by a regression of the manager's returns against the index's returns.

Rate of Return - Three different return numbers are usually quoted. The average rate of return is the simple average of the periodic returns. It is used in statistical calculations such as the standard deviation. The dollar-weighted rate of return (also referred to as the internal rate of return) is the rate of return that discounts a portfolio's terminal value and interim cash flows back to its initial value. It is the true rate of return that an investor receives on his or her initial and other periodic investments. The dollar-weighted return is considered misleading for performance-measurement purposes because the timing of periodic investment flows is considered outside the investment manager's control. The time-weighted rate of return adjusts for this by eliminating the effect of cash flows. It is the annualized compound rate of return achieved over a par-ticular period irrespective of cash flows. When measuring results since inception, most managers will have higher time-weighted returns than dollar-weighted returns. This is because performance usually suffers as additional assets are added. The two returns should also be considered when measuring past results and considering commitments to private investments such as venture capital. Historically, most of the good returns in these sectors have been achieved when the amount of capital committed has been small.

Return:
a. YTD: current NAV divided by December 31 NAV, minus 1.
b. 1 Year: current NAV divided by NAV 12 months prior, minus 1.
c. Multi-Year and Since-Inception Return: the percentage return such that if the beginning period NAV were to be compounded annually by that rate of return, it would equal current NAV.

Real Geometric Return - The compound growth rate in excess of inflation. The geo-metric return is often estimated by subtracting one-half the portfolio variance from the arithmetic return.

Real Return (Arithmetic) - The expected average annual return of the portfolio in excess of inflation.

Real Volatility - The expected annual standard deviation of returns.

Return/Standard Deviation - A measure indicating how much return has been generated per unit of risk as defined by standard deviation.

Return/Beta - Annual return divided by the estimated beta of the manager or index. A measure indicating how much return has been generated per unit of risk as defined by beta.

Risk - Exposure to uncertain change, either favorable or unfavorable. In popular usage, the focus is appropriately on adverse change. Annualized standard deviation is often used as a generic measurement of risk, but there are other, more complicated statistical measures. There are also investment risks that do not lend themselves to mathematical calculation, such as political risk.

Risk Premium - An additional required rate of return due to the extra risk incurred from investing in an asset class. Often, three-month U.S. Treasury bills are considered "risk free" investments and investors require no risk premium. Stocks are "risky" and investors require extra return above three-month T-bills to invest in them. This extra required return is the risk premium. Over time, the risk premium that investors require changes depending on the aggregate view of the market.

R-Squared - 1) The percentage of a portfolio's movement that is explained by movements in its benchmark index. A portfolio with an R-squared of 100 indicates that all of the portfolio's movements are completely explained by movements in the benchmark index. A portfolio must have an R-squared of 75 or higher for its alpha and beta to be considered reliable. 2) The proportion of the manager's return that can be explained by the index's return. A key indicator of how well an index fits a manager's investment style. For example, an R-squared of 0.93 means that 93% of the variation of the manager's return is explained by the index, and the rest is explained by other influences such as stock selection.

Serial Correlation (1-Month Lagged) - A measure of the correlation of a return series to itself over successive time intervals. In this case, how correlated the present month's return is to the historical prior month's. Less liquid strategies, and strategies that are marked-to-market infrequently or inaccurately, often exhibit serial correlation. Returns for relatively liquid strategies, such as those generated by investing in the S&P 500 or in equity market-neutral strategies, generally exhibit no serial correlation.

Sharpe Ratio - A risk-adjusted measure of return. The average of the periodic portfolio returns minus the periodic risk-free rate divided by the portfolio's standard deviation.

Short Sales - The sale of borrowed securities considered overvalued in order to purchase them later at lower prices to make a profit. Short selling can be used as a hedging technique or for speculation.

Skewness - A measure of symmetry in the distribution of returns. Positive skew implies that the right tail of the distribution is more pronounced than the left. In other words, relative to a symmetric distribution, the return series has some extreme high values. For a positively skewed distribution, the mean is higher than the median. The distribution of wealth in the United States is an example of a positively skewed distribution. With regard to hedge fund returns, negative skew—a distribution where the mean is below the median—implies that while the fund may have generally exhibited consistent positive returns, outsized events have been to the downside.

Sortino Ratio - A measure of excess return per unit of risk based on downside semi-variance, instead of total risk. While similar to the Sharpe Ratio, this ratio focuses only on downside volatility because investors are most concerned about the risk of loss.

Standard Deviation - A measurement of variation around a mean (the square root of the mean of the squared deviation of members of a population from the mean). The standard deviation is the most widely used proxy for risk. It is useful when the observations are normally distributed around the mean but can be misleading if they are not.

Target Fund Size - Target amount of aggregate commitments given in round numbers, such as $100 million or $1 billion.

Term - The period in years for which the fund is organized, usually 10 years, and the number of extensions at the discretion of the general partner or with the approval of the advisory committee.

Total Return - This time-weighted measure of performance includes both capital appreciation (or depreciation) and dividends or other income received.

Total Volatility (Standard Deviation) - The annualized standard deviation of the quarterly returns of the manager or index. A measure of the volatility of the returns of the portfolio. In any given year, there is a 66% chance that the manager's return will fall within plus or minus one standard deviation of the overall annual return.

Tracking Error - A measure of how much a portfolio deviates from its benchmark. Usually expressed as the standard deviation of the portfolio's excess return (alpha).

Win % - The percentage of months with returns above the return to T-Bills over the given time period.

Volatility - A measure of the dispersion or spread of observations around the mean. Statistically, this is expressed by the standard deviation. The words volatility and risk are often used interchangeably, although strictly speaking volatility is only one of several investment risks.

Volatility Above-Average Return - The annualized standard deviation of the quarterly returns that fall above the average quarterly return. A measure of the upside volatility of the returns.

Volatility Below-Average Return - The annualized standard deviation of the quarterly returns that fall below the average quarterly return. A measure of the downside volatility of the returns.

Worst Negative Quarter - The lowest quarterly return of the manager or index.

Worst Four Quarters - The lowest return over four consecutive quarters.

About the Authors

Nicole Wellmann Kraus, CFA, is the chief client officer at Strategic Investment Group. She oversees the development of client relationships and drives the firm's marketing strategy. She also serves as a member of Strategic's Board of Managers. Prior to that she spent nearly 12 years at SEI Investments working with endowments, pension funds, healthcare organizations, and foundations.

She has 27 years of experience in the Outsourced Chief Investment Office (OCIO) industry, having most recently served as director of institutional business at Hirtle, Callaghan & Co., where she attracted and serviced a broad range of clients. Before that she held various positions at SEI Investments Company working with OCIO clients. She has extensive experience advising investment committees, to whom she is often asked to provide insights on best practices and governance. Ms. Kraus serves on the Investment Advisory Subcommittee of the John Templeton Foundation. She also serves on the U.S. Impact Committee for 100 Women in Finance and as a mentor for Girls Who Invest.

She has also actively collaborated with the National Association of College and University Business Officers (NACUBO) for nearly a decade, including serving as a speaker at multiple NACUBO events. She is often asked to speak at AGB events. She has published various articles in the areas of investment committee governance and investment management. Additionally, Ms. Kraus is a frequent guest speaker and skillful moderator of investor panels at industry conferences.

She holds a B.A. in English and Computer Applications from the University of Notre Dame. She is a CFA charterholder and a member of the CFA Society of Washington, D.C.

Valentina Glaviano, CIMA®, managing director, is responsible for building new client relationships at Strategic Investment Group. She has over 35 years of experience working in investment management holding senior leadership positions at Guggenheim Investments, iShares, and Lazard Asset Management. She is a member of Strategic's diversity, equity, and inclusion working group, a cross-functional team that works to develop and retain diverse talent both within the firm and within the financial industry, to encourage and evaluate diversity within our sphere of influence (our firm, our managers, our vendors), and to foster an equitable and respectful work environment throughout the firm. Prior to joining Strategic, she was a director at Covariance Capital Management, formerly a subsidiary of TIAA Endowment & Philanthropic Services. At Covariance, Ms. Glaviano headed a business development effort to provide comprehensive OCIO services to non-profits with complex investment and risk-management needs.

She received a B.S. in Economics from the University of California at Los Angeles where she currently serves on the UCLA Department of Economics Board of Visitors. She is a Certified Investment Management Analyst ("CIMA®") professional. She has also been elected as a member of the International Women's Forum ("IWF"). IWF's members are elected by IWF leadership and include more than 7,000 diverse and accomplished women from 33 nations on six continents

Jay A. Yoder, CFA, brings multiple viewpoints to the analysis of endowment management. From 2006 to 2014, he served as investment committee chair (functionally the CIO) at Albright College. Despite its modest size (less than $100 million), Albright generated top-quartile returns and outperformed the average $1 billion+ endowment during his tenure. Albright was named Small Endowment of the Year by *Foundation & Endowment Money Management* in 2013.

Previously, Mr. Yoder spent a decade leading the investment office at two private liberal arts institutions—Vassar College, then Smith College. At both endowments, he wrote new investment policies, implemented modern portfolios with significant allocations to alternative investments, and generated peer- and benchmark-beating returns. He has also served as a member of, or advisor to, investment committees at three community foundations.

Mr. Yoder is now global strategy leader, natural resources for Mercer consulting, a MarshMcLennan company. He is the author of numerous articles and two other AGB publications: *The Investment Committee* (2011) and *Endowment Management: A Practical Guide* (2004).

Notes

1 Ochs, Joyce, "Staying Out of Trouble." *Pension Management*, Vol. 31, No. 9, 16–19.

2 Yale Investments Office, *The Yale Endowment Annual Report: 2002*, 14.

3 The endowment model is a concept of institutional investing that has won widespread recognition and is practiced, in particular, by larger endowments. It has three key tenets: 1) an equity bias ("own rather than loan"); 2) diversification (sometimes called "the only free lunch in investing"); and 3) an emphasis on illiquid investments (such as private capital) to pursue the return premium that should be associated with tying up one's capital over a multi-year period.

4 "Open architecture" refers to an option, offered by some firms, that allows clients to invest beyond that firm's lineup of external investment managers or in-house managers (sometimes referred to as a "platform"), but also in a wider range of competing firms' investment products.